PRAISE FOR
AN UNLIKELY PROPHET

". . . *a unique meditation on time and space, personal identity, and the creative instinct.*"

INDEPENDENT PUBLISHER

"*The finely crafted narrative will hold readers' attention, and the speculations in this 'spiritual autobiography' (as Schwartz calls it) will give even skeptics plenty of food for thought.*"

KEVIN GRANDFIELD, BOOKLIST

"*If you like comic books, especially* Superman, *and have an interest in Eastern spirituality,* An Unlikely Prophet *is the perfect book for you.*"

AMAZON.COM

"*An Unlikely Prophet is an essential text for anyone interested in the history of American comics, the principles behind fiction, and many of the themes Alan Moore has been exploring of late. Consider it 'Kavalier & Clay' meets the Superboy from Earth Prime.*"

RICH JOHNSON, COMIC BOOK RESOURCE

". . . *a can't-lay-it-down story. . . . It's all a great adventure, a book about 'possibilities.'*"

NAPRA REVIEW

". . . *a vast spiritual landscape with translucent forms from the past and future merging into physical form.*"

THE EDGE

"*Schwartz weaves a tale that lingers with you long after the read concludes. Symbolism, masked in the 'ordinary' details of Schwartz's life, is potently and subtly utilized.*"

BOB HUGHES, CONSCIOUSMEDIA.COM

A
GATHERING
OF SELVES

The Spiritual Journey
of the Legendary Writer of
Superman and Batman

ALVIN SCHWARTZ

Destiny Books
Rochester, Vermont

Destiny Books
One Park Street
Rochester, Vermont 05767
www.DestinyBooks.com

Destiny Books is a division of Inner Traditions International

Library of Congress Cataloging-in-Publication Data
Schwartz, Alvin, 1916–
  A gathering of selves : the spiritual journey of the legendary writer of Superman and Batman / Alvin Schwartz.
      p. cm.
  Summary: "Continuing on the Path without Form introduced in *An Unlikely Prophet,* Alvin Schwartz discovers the many selves that dwell within a being"—Provided by publisher.
  ISBN-13: 978-1-59477-109-5 (pbk.)
  ISBN-10: 1-59477-109-X (pbk.)
  1. Superman. 2. Spiritual life. 3. Cartoonists. 4. Buddhism. I. Title.
  PS3569.C5649G38 2006
  813'.54—dc22
                                                                    2006025741

Printed and bound in the United States by Lake Book Manufacturing

10 9 8 7 6 5 4 3 2 1

Text layout by Priscilla Baker
This book was typeset in Sabon, with Agenda used as a display typeface

To send correspondence to the author of this book, mail a first-class letter to the author c/o Inner Traditions • Bear & Company, One Park Street, Rochester, VT 05767, and we will forward the communication.

Tu ne me chercherais pas si tu ne m'avais trouvé.

You would not seek me if you had not found me.

—Pascal

Prologue

After almost two decades writing the world's two leading comic strips, *Superman* and *Batman,* I created *An Unlikely Prophet,* a personal memoir of my encounter with a mysterious Tibetan visitor named Thongden and how it led me to sublimate the mass superhero concept that had occupied my working life into its grander metaphysical significance. Mr. Thongden, a self-styled *tulpa*—a creature of pure thought and meditation—was the guide as I rode my private Superman fixation on a voyage of discovery, reaching out toward that inner awareness attained by the great metaphysical thinkers and mystics of East and West. It is on this note of positive anticipation that *An Unlikely Prophet* concludes. And that is where the events described in this volume begin.

A Gathering of Selves goes far beyond that earlier work. For instead of the personal enlightenment I might have expected through my strange, transforming encounter with Thongden, I began to suffer a new unrest. What I had originally experienced as a kind of higher understanding, promising peace or contentment, became a source of unrest and a strange new goad to pass beyond a state of passive awareness to one of action and participation.

Perhaps most startling in the events I describe here was the realization that I am not entirely the self I imagined myself to be, but a whole congeries of personalities living out their days in various realities, whose essential link lies in their specific common task—and the acceptance of a responsibility that is transpersonal and global in its reach.

This story carries us across the ordinary boundaries of the private personality, as well as the strictures of national boundaries and fixed timelines, as all of my other selves become enmeshed in a single cooperative action to ward off a fearsome threat to the ecological balance of the Earth herself. In this sequel, all the themes of *An Unlikely Prophet* are variously juxtaposed and a new, surprising link forged—the strange role of Batman, which I also wrote for many years, but with less heart than I gave to Superman. My experience of other selves allowed me finally to find and use the remarkable raw strength that the Batman experience had provided.

A Gathering of Selves carries the "enlightenment" experience to the next level of significance, the interpersonal level, revealing the wonders of connection with other sentient beings so that what we think of as "the self" becomes the foundation for the unity of all being.

Chapter One

I'm hardly the first one to go through an "awakening" experience only to discover that instead of finding myself living easy by coasting along the gentle slopes of expanded insight, I was plunged into a new restlessness. A strange kind of hunger filled my days. I struggled to find the meaning of an indefinable longing and an emptiness in the face of all activities that were no more than soothing or pleasurable. I had tasted something else, and the provisions of the world I knew had, as a consequence, lost their savor. I was discovering that an enlargement of consciousness comes at some peril: a sense of permanent loss, even a kind of clinical depression, unless one continues along the same tenuous path that brought the enlargement about. But how was I to do that? The only one who could really help me was Thongden. Had he started it all and then abandoned me? It seemed that way. I had no idea where Thongden was and had no reason to feel I would ever encounter him again. I knew that I was, to put it mildly, in a very difficult situation.

To my wife, Kay, who suffered through the transforming events of my encounter with Thongden, it was clearly a spiritual experience. I thought so too. But I also thought something else was now part of the story, a kind of responsibility that I didn't yet fully understand.

Something that I had to do was still waiting to be done. Something that I owed, somehow.

I had tried to come to grips with this new sense of responsibility by telling the story in *An Unlikely Prophet*. But that work had simply recapitulated the whole experience, bringing me to a point where I discovered that there were still vaster depths to plumb. And what led to this discovery was something that, on the face of it, seemed very remote from parallel universes or any possible role in the enlargement of consciousness. I'm talking about money.

That's it, money. Mammon! Presumably the very antithesis of the spiritual. And yet, as Franz Kafka once wrote, "The ground by which you fall becomes the means to lift you up."

So this work begins with money and ends with . . . what? Well, for one thing, I assumed a responsibility I never thought I could handle. It was almost like carrying the world on my back. But, on the other hand, there was help. Yes, and perhaps even more astonishing, that help arose out of my very own self.

Like many investors in early 1994, I anticipated a continuation of the rapid growth of the Mexican economy, so I bought into a Latin American mutual fund. Then there was the revolt in Chiapas. Then, the devaluation of the peso, and the collapse of the Mexican Bolsa. I lost forty thousand dollars. It didn't wipe us out—but it hurt. It made a difference in our lifestyle.

But it wasn't just that particular loss that bothered my wife. It was the fact that it was not an isolated incident. I'd been losing constantly, even in situations where almost everyone else was winning.

"The problem is," Kay told me, "that I think you want to lose. You never really were comfortable about money, so you work hard to let go of it. It's not a problem in financial judgment. I think it's a psychological problem."

I protested. "A psychological problem? Me? Why would I be psychologically fixated on losing money?"

Kay just turned her soft luminous look on me. "After forty years, we're supposed to be each other's extra eyes, remember? You see things about me that I can't see. And I do the same for you."

"And you see me punishing myself by losing money?"

"Punishing us," she said tersely.

"I don't agree," I insisted. "This Latin American thing came as a real surprise to the whole financial community."

"Which means you're getting ready to do it again."

I shrugged. "So what do you suggest? Can we arbitrate this?"

"You can go talk to Steve. If you do that, I'll stay out of it."

"You're that convinced?" I said. "You think Steve will agree with you?"

"Go see," she said.

We'd been together too long for me not to realize that arguing would simply lead to an impasse. So I decided to follow her suggestion and call in our personal outside expert. I would consult Steve Jordan, expecting that in the end he'd help me convince Kay that her concern for my psychological state was vastly exaggerated.

Steve Jordan would be the natural one to consult, because at the time of this conversation we were staying at our winter home in Merritt Island, Florida, right next to Cocoa Beach. Steve and his wife, Johanna, our close friends for thirty-five years, lived only a half hour away in Orlando, where they had settled permanently after leaving New York over two decades back. Steve had gotten his doctorate long ago and had been a practicing psychotherapist for thirty years now. He had established a reputation for, among other things, his work with autistic children.

Kay and I, the perpetual snowbirds, managed to spend some time with the Jordans every winter when we settled into our Florida quarters. If I had to discuss any kind of psychological problem with anyone, it would have to be with Steve first, since we were that close. And of course, I'd count on him to recommend someone for me. And if he were to tell Kay she was overworking the psychological angle, she'd accept it from him. At least, that's what I was expecting would happen.

The problem was that in all our very intimate personal exchanges, Kay and I had never discussed with either Steve or Johanna what had happened to me last year. We had never exchanged a word with them about Thongden. Of course, by now, the first half of my manuscript for *An Unlikely Prophet* had been sent to him. I was in the habit of sending early stages of important work to the Jordans, and they must have had a chance to read it, but we weren't sure. Neither of them had said a word to us about it. Not even a phone call. Well, now was a chance to get into that too. In fact, if I were to consult Steve, we'd have to get into it. If I had any psychological problem, it would have had to be connected with all of those strange happenings described in the first half of the book.

I called Steve and made an appointment to see him, sort of professionally. During this phone conversation, he again said nothing about *An Unlikely Prophet,* although I gave him several openings. He scheduled a time, and I drove to his home in Orlando the next day.

"Actually," Steve said, when I got there, "I did read your manuscript."

"And you never said a word to me about it?"

"I figured we'd be getting together pretty soon, so I waited with my questions."

We were sitting at a small table on his glassed-in porch, which had a fireplace that was never used because it always smoked. The natives called such a porch a Florida Room. Steve called it his gab chamber. He was wearing a white shirt and a pair of well-cut shorts that somehow looked frumpy on him. He was a big, perpetually rumpled man of sixty with black eyes and a graying black beard and hair.

When he walked, his movement was loose and careless. When he sat, he seemed to be haphazardly distributed in his chair. Physically, he was inalterably and hopelessly sloppy. Just the obverse of his mind. That side of him was precise, perceptive, and unerringly sly.

"What questions?" I asked.

He got up and stood looking out across the wide ragged lawn, broken by clumps of colorful exotic shrubs that Johanna had planted over the years. Everything was in full bloom.

"First, was it all true? No fiction added, no flights of fancy?"

"All true. Maybe it's the *tulpa* you're worried about? Thongden?"

Steve turned back to me. "A *tulpa*," Steve declared, as though reading from some invisible text, "is a human being generated by thought rather than through normal channels, such as the birth canal. No, the existence of your Tibetan *tulpa* friend, Thongden, was something I could go along with. In fact, when I first started your book, it occurred to me that you were having more trouble accepting him than I'd have had."

"I didn't know you were a secret New Ager," I said with muted asperity.

He laughed at me and sat down. "Listen, I've had at least three patients over the years who are born-agains. They didn't know it, perhaps, but they were all basically Marianists. One of them particularly, I remember, used to pray for long hours in front of an icon of Mary at her church. She told me how she'd envisage every detail of that icon—the flowing blue robes, the golden hair, the pink face, the loving expression. Then, after a time, at home, she began to receive visitations from Mary. She didn't tell her family, but this Mary wasn't like any dream. And I don't think I could really say my client was in a hypnogogic state. Besides, Mary often gave her good advice about what to do, contrary to what my client herself would have done. Also, at one point, this, well, *tulpa,* if you like, of Mary, actually embraced her. And she insists it was a warm, solid embrace."

"Why did she come to you for treatment then?" I asked.

"You see?" Steve said triumphantly. "You're not as ready to accept my *tulpa* story as I am to accept yours. The patient had a child with asthma, and she thought she might have been a causative factor. In fact, it was Mary who advised her to consult a psychologist. Okay?"

"Well," I said. "Okay. So my experience wasn't unique, then."

Again a smile from Steve. "Come on, Al. How could it be unique? Do you know the story of the mystical appearance of the Virgin of Fatima and the bizarre events that followed? This goes all the way back to 1917. Seventy thousand people saw the image. Or all the dozens of other mass sightings of religious figures around the world before and since then? And how about UFOs? At the least, we're seeing pretty powerful proof of the ability of the mind to mold reality into a thousand different forms. So why should your Thongden be so special?"

"All right," I said, lifting my hands. "Nothing to it. Happens every day. So why am I making such a big thing of it?"

"Then don't," Steve said, smiling at me in an odd way. "Actually, it is fairly common. I mean, the ability of mind to influence and shape matter. Trouble is, most people, including scientists, find it too troubling to think about seriously. So they pretend it doesn't happen."

I looked at him in amazement. "Have you ever met a *tulpa*?"

He shook his head. "I don't think so. But, how would I really know? I mean, your friend Thongden turns up at your house and informs you that even Alexander Hamilton was a *tulpa*. Given Hamilton's mostly unknown personal history, why not? Maybe there are more of them around. I wouldn't know. My experience is limited to my patients. But I do know about people who can bend metal with their thoughts. You know, the Uri Geller effect. I even have a couple of teenage patients who can do that. Not to mention a few poltergeist materializations. All in a day's work, you might say. And I'm familiar with various effects of mental energies on altering random number sequences. And better yet, with the idea that matter itself may be much more a subjective than an objective reality, at least according to some very reputable quantum physicists who think that electrons only exist because our imaginations created them. And then there's the anthropic principle."

"What's that?"

"Oh, sorry. It's the idea that our presence as intelligent observers is in some manner a factor in the existence of the universe. Quite a respectable scientific notion these days. So, really, how much of a jump is that to a *tulpa*?" He ran his fingers through his beard and watched me with a kind of faint amusement. "By the way, would you like coffee? Or some tea?"

I shook my head in an impatient negative. "Then you believe me?"

"My believing anything doesn't accredit it," he said. "But as Freud might have asked, what's the epinosic gain? What do you accomplish for yourself by making it up?"

Our conversation went on like that for perhaps another twenty minutes. He even managed to admit that he'd enjoyed reading *An Unlikely Prophet* and wondered how much further I'd be taking it. I told him I didn't know. I only knew I wasn't finished with it yet, but wasn't ready to go on at this time. It was as though some kind of grace I'd been expecting hadn't yet materialized. So I was waiting. I also told him about Kay's theory that my losing money was a psychological issue.

As we talked on, Steve mentioned that there had been many times in his life when he became aware for a few unforgettable moments of the pure grace of being, but that was balanced for him by the existence of what he called "dark forces."

"What dark forces?" I asked.

Steve was evasive. "The term isn't mine, really. I picked it up from someone I met within the past couple of years, a man who impressed me very much. But that's something else."

Then he insisted that we get into my reason for coming to see him, my post-Thongden depression, as he called it.

"I don't like the sound of that," I said. "It's not quite right."

"I wasn't describing it. I was placing it. But fine, you describe it."

"Dreariness," I said. "Everything seems dreary, empty, not worth thinking about. Did it ever occur to you that hell is just a gray place?"

"I don't suppose you ever, during your theological meanderings, read St. John the Divine?"

"You mean, his dark night of the soul?"

"Isn't that what you're talking about? You had a glimpse of something beyond the everyday. An intimation far beyond your everyday reality. It fascinated you. It thrilled you. Dazzled you, probably. Isn't that it?"

"All right. So why should all that lead to . . ." I spread my arms in a melancholy gesture, ". . . to this?"

"Why not? Why wouldn't you feel that way after being dropped back into the dullness of ordinary life? You're a prisoner, condemned for life. Suddenly, you get a vision, maybe even a promise of freedom, that stuns and fascinates you. And then the gates slam shut again. That would bother me. In fact, it would drive me crazy. But don't take my word for it. Almost all the great mystics have had the same experience. They get this vision of wonders beyond their wildest dreams, and then it's snatched away. So what do they do? Mostly, they're plunged into despair. They try to struggle back. But it's a massive effort. A terrible, unimaginable wrestling with a force beyond their understanding. Like Jacob and the angel."

"I've thought about all that stuff," I admitted gloomily. "But these days there aren't any angels around to wrestle with. I thought you might have a better idea."

"Like what? A prescription for Prozac? Would you settle for that?"

"No."

"Then how can I help you?"

"That's what I'm asking you."

Steve was thoughtful for a while. He kept studying me, sitting on the other side of the table and drumming his fingers from time to time. Finally he said, "This man I mentioned earlier . . ."

"What man?"

"The one I referred to, when I said I got the term *dark forces* from him."

"What about him?"

". . . Besides," Steve added ruminatively, "I wouldn't be the one to treat you, no matter what I thought."

"But you think I should see someone?"

Steve shrugged. "Well, certainly not me. You'd need someone who'd been where you were. At least that."

I was standing now. I leaned across the table. "You know someone who's had a similar experience?"

"I'm not sure," Steve said. "Except that he seemed to know about such things."

"Know, how? You also know. What's so special about this guy? Who is he?"

Steve rose suddenly. "How about I go get us some coffee?"

I nodded. "Sure, coffee."

He went off into the kitchen and for five minutes I sat there staring furiously out the window. By the time he got back with the coffee, I had come to some sort of decision.

"I don't really think," I began tentatively, "that there's anyone around I can talk to. Not after the kind of experiences I've had recently. I mean, with you, it's different. But as you've said yourself often enough, most of your colleagues don't really know which way is up."

Steve fixed my coffee for me, the way he knew I drank it.

Aspartame and 1 percent milk. Then he slid the cup toward me. "Up until a year ago, I'd have agreed with you," he admitted. "But there's this new boy in town. I think he's done some very interesting work. Also, he's got an approach that's more up your alley. As I said, he knows something about dark forces. Doesn't sound very psychological, I know. But, in fact, without those forces, we wouldn't need psychology."

"That's strange talk from you."

"We all grow, in our own ways." He gave me an odd smile. "Do you want to hear more?"

"I'm listening."

"He reads auras."

He looked at me questioningly as he said this, as though some momentary hesitation had intervened.

"Yes?" I said. There was a lot more than doubt in the way I uttered the word.

"This person, I don't know him intimately. But we've met on a number of occasions and talked for several hours at a time." Steve paused to sip at his coffee. "He came up to Miami from the Argentines, just after the Falklands War. Last year, he moved to the Orlando area. Interesting background. Looks partly *indios*. Probably is. In fact, some of his notions are kind of shamanistic. But he's impressive. Hard to forget. Also, I sent a few patients to him myself. Hispanics mostly, whom I thought he'd serve better in their own language. And he turned out to be remarkably effective, in my opinion."

"I'm not exactly Hispanic," I said.

"I know, but, as soon as I started to think about your *tulpa* experience . . ."

"Yes?" I said again, growing impatient as he began to hesitate.

"He's almost as strange as you are," Steve added, breaking into a wry smile. "Maybe that's why I got interested in him. Also . . ." Again, a pensive expression accompanied by a long pause before he added, "there's almost a kind of synchronicity. You know what I'm talking about?"

"No," I said.

He pulled himself from his chair, strode to the glassed inside wall of the room, and peered out at the wilderness of plants his wife had established around the building where it touched the edge of the lawn. "Well, it is strange that this particular individual should instantly pop into my mind the moment you turn up needing someone. Wouldn't you call that a meaningful coincidence?"

"And you really think I should see someone?" I challenged again.

"Only if he happens to be able to read auras." He laughed as he said it, but I knew he was referring to the way Thongden had managed to see various fragmentary images around me, which might be considered a more refined form of aura reading. That latter normally consists of an ability to see the electromagnetic radiations that extend from the human form. A skilled aura reader can then interpret a person's state of health and mind from the various auric colors and their degree of saturation. A crude form of what Thongden actually did with me.

"By the way, what happened to Thongden?" Steve asked unexpectedly.

I shook my head. "I'm not too clear about it. The best I can figure out is that in absorbing my Superman phantasm, I absorbed Thongden along with it. So, at the very least, something of him is still with me."

"Why? Does it make you feel different?"

"Not in any Thongdenish way I can think of. Do I seem different to you?"

"Well," Steve shrugged. "It's hard for me to judge so soon. How can I put it? I get a feeling that you've lost a certain wispiness that was part of your charm, but probably detracted from—no, wait. Let's say, you seem more focused. A lot more. In fact, I'm even kind of surprised at how your mind seems to have quieted down. Normally, you'd be discussing three or four different subjects all at once."

"You call that an improvement? It's probably just depression."

"Come on. It's only a quick read," Steve said, hedging a bit.

"But this sudden drop into despair, after reaching such heights? You think he'd understand that?"

"All I have to go on is, well, let's call it instinct. The thing that always works for me when I do therapy. You'll find him interesting. I'm sure of that. Why not try him?"

Chapter Two

The man's name was Tohanda. Steve gave me his address and phone number and I went away saying I'd talk it over with Kay and think about it some more. Except I didn't discuss it with Kay at all. I just sat around and thought about it for two days. And then I got this call for a four-hour appearance on a nationally syndicated radio show to talk about my years of work on Superman. Kay was excited—until I told her I wasn't up to doing it.

"Why not?"

"Because I don't have a vantage point to discuss it from anymore. For a while, I thought I did. And then this whole thing caught up with me. I not only have no answers, I don't really care. Not from where I stand now."

The next day, I called Tohanda's number and talked to his secretary, mentioning Steve's recommendation, and she set me up with a morning appointment for two days later. All I told Kay was that I was going to see a guy Steve had recommended. She didn't ask me anything more, since she could see that I didn't want to discuss it at that point. I spent the next day and a half wondering why I'd allowed myself to be talked into something just because Steve had a vague hunch I'd find this guy helpful.

As it turned out, Tohanda's office was located roughly halfway between my home and Steve's, about ten miles east of Orlando and already into Brevard County. I took the Beeline, cut over to Route 520, and headed east. In less than twenty minutes, I drove into a village that consisted of little more than a roadside strip mall. Just beyond, I found a well-graveled artery that led off on the right to a sprawling cinder block house all decked out with bright orange ceramic roof tiles, a mailbox at the driveway with the name Tohanda, and not a neighbor any closer than maybe seven hundred feet. A ragged phalanx of red and white oleanders lined the driveway and escorted me almost to the garage door. I stopped about twenty feet from it, walked to the front porch, and banged the heavy knocker on the entrance door.

I waited a full two minutes before anyone came to open up. And then I laughed and said to the broad flat familiar face that stood just back of the threshold, "I understand you read auras." From the tone of my voice, I might just as well have said to him, "I understand you sell grapefruit." I sounded bland, somewhat formal and detached. A state of shock can manifest itself in the most ordinary way.

Over a year had passed since I'd last seen Thongden. I hadn't expected to see him again. I was convinced that I'd somehow absorbed him into myself, along with other strange projections of my imagination. In spite of what Steve had said, I was beginning to doubt that Thongden had ever really been more than that, salutary though the experience had been. But here he was once more—which was patently impossible. Because at the very time I had presumably been visiting him at his home in midtown Manhattan last year, he would also have had to be here in Florida, treating patients and getting to know Steve Jordan. And at the same time he had been doing such an effective job on those Hispanic patients Steve had sent to him, he'd also been escorting me around the Bronx Zoo and inducting me into the remarkable and revealing technique of consciousness transference through a variety of Eastern esoteric breathing techniques.

"Nice to see you again," Thongden said. He nodded, offered me a courteous smile, and motioned me inside.

"Maybe you just commuted, is that it?" I said, knowing as I spoke that the answer, if any, lay much deeper than that. For one thing, he looked different. He wasn't quite as tall, and his features had somehow grown more Caucasian. There was less of the inner epicanthic fold around his eyes, and his cheekbones had lost a certain flatness and protruded more. Even his hair was lighter. He could almost have been what the anthropologists call a mixed dolichocephalic type, as though he had Scandinavian ancestry not many generations back. And yet, it was still unmistakably he.

"That must have been Jordan," he said, waving me on inside.

"What about Jordan?"

"He told you I read auras."

He had led me into a room that was a more-than-adequate replication of a proper psychotherapist's waiting room, with a vaulted ceiling and comfortable chairs grouped around a large TV. Before this, it must have been someone's living room. Playing softly in the background, there was even some soothing white noise that passed for music. And a magazine rack filled with outdated popular periodicals. Thongden had always had a great feeling for detail.

"Isn't that the way you planned it?" I said.

Thongden shrugged. The gesture was all too familiar and brought a flood of memories pouring back. "Not completely. I'm not here on your account. Not at all. Let's say it just worked out that way."

He motioned me to a seat on one of the chairs, and settled into one facing me.

"I really am practicing psychotherapy," he explained. "And as I'm sure Dr. Jordan told you, I do have other patients." He looked the part well enough. He even wore a white coat, as though he needed to reassure himself of his own authenticity. Then, surprisingly, he said again but more specifically this time, "I'm not here because you're in Florida. It's the other way round. You're in Florida because of me."

By now, of course, I was familiar with the kind of games he played. But I went along. "How do you explain that, when I didn't even know you were still . . ."

"Alive?"

"—an independent entity," I corrected.

He shrugged. "We'll get to that in proper time. But for now, let's deal with your problem. Let's go inside, to my examining room." He rose, and seeing that I hadn't followed, he looked back questioningly.

"Do we really have to go through this whole charade?" I said.

"No, no. The light's better in there. This waiting room won't do at all."

"And what am I supposed to call you? Tohanda? What about Thongden?"

"Not yet," he said cryptically. "Come along." He gestured for me to follow.

I got up in spite of myself, still protesting. "Better for what?" I was referring to his remark about the examining room, of course.

I heard a smothered sound of laughter from him as he started toward the doorway leading deeper into the house. "For reading auras—what else?"

Thongden resisted all of my efforts to get him to explain himself or his presence or even his remark that my being in Florida was because of him. He insisted on getting right down to the business of a preliminary examination, as he called it, based on what I'd told his secretary.

The light was certainly different in this room. It had a dim, gray, diffuse sort of radiance that spread evenly across everything, originating from a single opalescent panel on the far wall. Other than that, there was nothing but a large, plain square desk with a swivel chair, and a pair of small upholstered chairs for visitors. These spartan furnishings were themselves a flat gray that rendered them barely visible in that light. But Thongden stood out clearly in that ambience, as I presume I did myself.

He asked me to assume a stiff upright position on one of the visitors' chairs, then quietly stared at me. Actually, he stared at the space just above my left shoulder, the way he had done on several occasions not so long ago up in New York, when he'd come to me after losing his creator, the late Everett Nelson.

"You don't see any Superman phantasms around me anymore, do you?" I asked, trying a more oblique approach to eliciting some explanations.

"Oh, no. That was cleared up very nicely, thanks to the extra pressure I put on you at the time."

"Then you really did cause the collapse of that carnival ride!" I said, half rising from the chair. I was referring to that incident in which I imagined myself to be on a carnival high ride whose sudden collapse caused me to envision myself as Superman and bring about a wholesale rescue of all the passengers, including myself.

"Of course. And please try to keep your position."

I settled back. "At first, I thought it was a malicious streak breaking out in you. But I finally realized your purpose was therapeutic. Especially since the carnival thing never really happened."

"You must learn to distinguish among dimensions. It happened to you, didn't it? Anyway, thank you for giving me the benefit of the doubt," he said, squinting more concentratedly now at that area over my left shoulder where he had first discovered a small but clear Superman phantasm, indicating that I had some unsolved business with my past as a comics writer.

"Don't tell me I've still got other stuff hanging around," I said.

"Oh, we never quite get rid of everything. There are always thought fragments of some sort that linger around us. But . . . well, you seem to be clear of anything that I'd consider important—almost."

"What do you mean, *almost?*"

He shook his head and frowned. "That's what I'm trying to understand," he said, sounding genuinely puzzled. "There's a form of some sort there that I can't quite resolve. It's blurred, out of focus, you see? But it's too strong to be unimportant. Isn't there something you've been preoccupied with?"

"Well, there's that thing about losing money, Kay thinks."

"I mean, something you've been carrying around for years. Maybe decades."

I frowned. "Why? Was it there before? I mean this blurry thing you're looking at."

"I'm not sure. The Superman phantasm was so strong, it tended to overshadow everything else. Also, maybe your own thinking about whatever this is hadn't cleared up enough to give it visibility."

"So what do we do about it?" I said.

"We clear it up, of course."

His method, as I should have remembered from past experience, was through special breathing exercises. He had me face the wall opposite the luminous panel and stare at it while he instructed me in one of his special patterns of *nadi-sudi*, breathing in through one nostril while holding the other, then reversing the procedure, then changing the length of inspirations and expirations so that the alternate breathing technique acquired a unique and rather rapid rhythm. I didn't know exactly how long he had me keep this up but my vision was beginning to get overwhelmed by bright flashes and my head felt uncomfortably light. It seemed to me that I'd been practicing for about ten minutes or so, when I felt I couldn't do anymore. It was about then that he suddenly told me to stop and resume normal breathing. Then he informed me I'd been at it for over two hours.

While I was trying to digest that startling fact and allowing myself to slowly drift back to feeling normal, I began to notice that he was staring past my left shoulder again.

"It's much clearer," he announced. "We've got a sharp fix on your phantasm now. A man in his early forties, I'd say. Dark haired, high clear forehead, keen alert expression, and kind of a perpetual tense stare. Wears a conventional business suit, but appears to be compact and powerfully built underneath it. Also, seems to have what you Americans call a high-pressure personality. A lot of unresolved anger as well. Any idea who it is?"

I shook my head. "None at all. I can't think of anyone I know like that."

"He's obviously what you'd call a driven type. Gives off a sense of command. And wealth. But there's a glaring inconsistency—he seems to favor a blue suit and a white shirt that's not too au courant these days. Also, for a wealthy business executive, the suit is a kind of high-saturation cobalt blue that wouldn't look right in any board-room. Does that stir any associations?"

"White shirt and blue suit, a sort of deep medium blue?"

"Actually, kind of bright blue."

"Do the features again," I said.

"Square jawed, very regular features. Almost resembles what used to be called a collar ad type. In fact, I'd have thought he was a model except for that obviously driven and commanding presence."

"Hmm . . . flashy blue suit and square jaw. Almost like a caricature."

"Or a cartoon?" Thongden suggested.

"Cartoon? Business suit? Square jaw." I laughed. "Sounds like a comic strip version of something. Even, well, Bruce Wayne. Other-wise, I don't know. I give up."

"Who's Bruce Wayne?"

"Oh, he's . . . he's the real identity of—" I grabbed at the sides of my face with one hand and stared at Thongden, miming a sense of sudden revelation.

"Yes?"

"Batman."

"Aah."

"Why do you say *aah*? Why in the world would I be developing a phantasm of Bruce Wayne after all these years?"

"Maybe you should tell me. What does Bruce Wayne do when he's not being Batman? I'm not up on comics, except for what I've learned from you."

"What does Bruce do? Nothing much. He behaves like a wealthy playboy to most of the world, but, he's also supposed to be a shrewd financier. That's the way I always saw him anyhow. Mostly, not very interesting." I frowned. "But let's say it *is* Bruce Wayne. Why would I—?"

Thongden had moved around to the other side of his desk and settled into his swivel chair. Folding his hands on the desktop, he leaned toward me. "You thought of him as a financier?"

"Well, after all the years I spent writing the comic strip in which he was supposed to be a financier, how else should I have thought of him?"

"But that's really what you came to see me about, isn't it, my dear fellow," he commented in a tone of mocking politeness. He steepled his fingers together and rested his chin on them as he gazed at me. "Your problem with finances?"

I sat there unable to say a word, trying to think my way through a growing state of confusion.

"I seem to remember your telling me that between Batman and Superman, you favored Superman," Thongden said. "You worked as much on Batman, but for some reason, you never developed the same level of interest in him. Do you remember telling me that?"

"Of course. And it's true. Superman intrigued me because of the way he represented a kind of degraded messianic symbolism. Batman was just kind of an old pulp character translated into comic book form. I wrote a lot of Batman stories, and probably did the good ones with as much zest as I did Superman. But apart from doing the job, I always felt Superman meant something more than that."

"And so he did," Thongden said. "But then, why would you blur Bruce Wayne like that, and yet build a solid phantasm out of him and carry it around all these years? What made him become a problem you couldn't shake off?"

I shrugged and remained silent.

"Remember, it wasn't Batman you made a phantasm of. It was Bruce Wayne. Why?"

"That part is simple enough. Because Bruce was the reality and Batman the disguise. In Superman's case, he was real. Clark Kent was the disguise."

"Also, you apparently have a very blurry idea of your own finances, and so, your phantasm of Bruce Wayne, the financier, is also blurry."

"Wow," I said mockingly, "that's a real slick connection. Maybe a little too slick?"

"Well, you could have thought of Wayne as a playboy socialite, which got more emphasis in the strip than his financial persona. No, your Bruce Wayne is a little different than the comics version."

"I thought you just told me you didn't know much about comics."

"I don't. But I can read you. Besides, you're evading the question."

Again I shrugged. "To me, Bruce Wayne couldn't have pretended to be a playboy socialite unless he was fundamentally a skillful financial man."

"Really?"

And suddenly, I'd had enough of the whole thing. Why was I letting him lead me on? What was he really up to? Why was he here?

How had he arranged to have me show up here too, and what was he planning to use me for? And Steve Jordan too, for that matter. How was he using Steve? I let it all come pouring out of me in the form of angry questions as I jumped up from my chair and insisted that he explain. "And furthermore," I added, "I'm not so sure your destroying that carnival ride in the Bronx was really for such a benign purpose after all. So either you tell me everything, or I walk. I have no intention of functioning in a situation where I'm up to my ears in mysteries, Doctor Tohanda."

"Aah," he said, grinning. "Only a couple of hours and already we've got the Bruce Wayne side of you emerging." He proceeded to stifle my protest with a wave of the hand. "But, all right. Sit down. I intended to tell you anyway before you left. So now's about right."

Chapter Three

I could tell that Kay knew at once, after I got home late that afternoon, that something very unusual had happened to me. I didn't try to hide it, exactly. It was just that I needed time to find a way of telling her. I hadn't fully digested it all myself.

"I called Steve," she told me.

"Okay."

This was some fifteen minutes after my arrival during which time I hadn't said anything more enlightening than "Hello."

"Okay? Is that all you have to say?"

"No. I'm thinking about it."

As I spoke, I walked toward the patio doors to peer at a blue heron that had planted itself on the lawn just beyond the screened porch of our ground floor condo. "George is back," I announced, abruptly changing the subject.

In the background, the Banana River pulsated within a soggy gray haze. It was barely possible to see the mainland emerging along the western shore. Kay followed behind me, walking slowly onto the patio in order not to frighten the big bird away. "That's not George," she announced after a careful inspection.

"How do you know?" I stood with my back to her, a few feet away.

"Because George has a skinned look around one leg where it joins his body. This one doesn't. It's a younger bird. Maybe even one of George's offspring. You remember he mated last year?"

"Oh, I forgot."

"I called Steve," she began again, still standing behind me. "Because you were so long getting back, I got worried. He said he sent you to see someone."

"Yes," I said, turning around and facing her. "A Dr. Tohanda."

"Yes?"

"Only it wasn't Dr. Tohanda at all. It was Thongden."

"Thongden?" she repeated in a single rising breath. "Your old *tulpa*? *That* Thongden?" She looked stricken, her hands partially raised, palms outward, with the fingers curled just a little inward as though she'd started reaching for something and then suddenly lost sight of it.

"Yes. That Thongden. But not exactly my old *tulpa*. I mean, he presented himself out of—" I shook my head. "I don't know exactly how to say this, but he was out of a different time frame. From before I met him last year."

She came closer, took me by the hand and led me inside and got me to sit on the living room sofa. She sat beside me.

"Don't analyze it. Just tell me what happened, step by step. Starting with Steve."

So I told her everything: from the time I walked into Steve's, how I spent two days mulling over whether I should follow his recommendation, and then how I showed up at Tohanda's place and found Thongden again. And how he uncovered what he called my Bruce Wayne syndrome. And then I gathered myself to tell Kay the part I still wasn't sure I believed myself.

"This is going to be hard for you," Thongden had warned, when he began his revelations. He had led me out of the examining room so that we could settle more comfortably in the waiting room. There were no other patients present and I assumed that if he'd had any other appointments during that time, he had probably canceled them.

"Yes, it'll be hard," he continued, "because you're caught in the one-way event sequence, otherwise known as linear time. A *tulpa* like myself understands that that's no more than a product of human consensus. A 'modal category of conception' according to your respected nineteenth-century Western philosopher, Immanuel Kant. In reality, of course, everything is really happening at once." I was again enjoying that strange capacity for heightened recall I usually experienced when Thongden was around. I seemed able to replicate our conversation almost word for word.

"A modal—what?" Kay interrupted.

"Kant, the German philosopher with the sesquipedalian phraseology," I said, with a deprecatory smile.

"I know that one, at least. Means a foot and a half long."

"Good. Can we get back to Thongden now?"

"You bet," she said archly, using what, to her Canadian ear, always sounded like a quaintly American phrase.

"Well . . . as I said, our notion of time, according to Thongden, is only a product of human consensus. Everything is really happening at once."

"I've heard that before, but I don't understand it."

"Nobody understands it except, well, abstractly. Through mathematics. Can I go on anyway? He did have a kind of interesting explanation. But that's not what shook me up. Remember way back when he came to me because, he said, Nelson—the scholar who created him by long meditation back in Tibet—Nelson had died and he needed me to think about him?"

"Do you think I'll ever forget?"

"All right, then. Try to wind your mind around this one."

She squeezed her eyes shut in a comic grimace and said, "I'm ready."

"Well, Nelson isn't dead. He's still communicating with Thong-den. But—" Here I raised a forefinger for dramatic emphasis. "Way back when Thongden first came to visit me and asked for my help, Nelson really had died. So how come he's alive now? Easy. In *that* now, when Thongden first came to the house, Nelson had died. But in *this* now, Nelson is still alive because this now predates *our* now by thirteen years. It doesn't make sense? Okay, then listen. This is how Thongden explains it. He says that in actual fact, when I absorbed my Superman phantasm after I used him to save us from the collapse of that carnival ride, I also absorbed Thongden who, by then, had become my *tulpa*, since I had taken over from Nelson. Okay?"

I saw she was about to interrupt, so I raised a finger again. "Wait. But currently, or in *this* now, Thongden is not absorbed, because for him, this now is neither before nor after the events of last year. In his sense, the two nows are on a parallel track. So that, while we can remember a future that exists in the past, we've just got the order wrong because our minds work in a one-way linear direction. All right, that's what he told me. And, as I'm sure you're feeling, he left me totally confused. It didn't help when he also tried to explain it was really a quantum event."

"Fine," Kay said. "I'm confused. So far we're in agreement."

"Then Thongden said to me, 'Think of it like this. You and I are like two mathematical points. We're contiguous to each other in time. But there's no timeline. Why? Because two points don't make a line. You have to have a third point in between. It takes three points to make a line.' So I said, 'Where then does the third point come in?' And he said, 'It doesn't. You invent it. You do that to support your beliefs. In reality, it isn't there. Where there are just two points, the contiguity can take place in any direction, there's nothing to limit or define it. It can be past, present, future. But since you're caught in the time stream, you have to position it in a strict linear order.'

"Then he gave me a funny look and said, 'Such odd juxtapositions of time are common enough in dreams. Why must you feel that they can't exist in the dream of physical life?' "

Kay thought about it for a while. She didn't stir from her seat. "In reality," she repeated, almost to herself, "there's no timeline. So," she looked up at me. "Where are we?"

"Oh no you don't," I said. "You're not getting me into that one."

She then seemed to go off on a different tack. "Ever since Thongden first showed up, our nice stable world seems to have shifted completely out of focus. I mean, Alvin, where are we? And what happens next?"

"That at least I can answer. You can only be at the place where the thread can be followed. That's how you keep your direction. Now, my thread—and remember, you started this thing—is to find out why I have problems with money. So far, we know it has something to do with Bruce Wayne. That is, the way Bruce Wayne took shape in my mind while I was writing Batman. So far, we discovered a connection between my somewhat cloudy feelings about the Bruce Wayne character and the fact that he was a financier. At least, I saw him as a financier. The next step, according to Thongden, is for me to better understand my image of Bruce Wayne along with his Batman alter ego. I agreed to go back and let Thongden lead me through the whole thing. But this time, he wants me to plan to be away for a while. Do you think you can put up with my absence for a few days?"

"If it has to be that way, of course."

"He also said that this time again, like the last, there's a bit of quid pro quo involved. If he helps me resolve my problem, I have to agree to help with his."

"And what problem is that?"

"I don't know. That's what I feel a little uneasy about."

Again, it was Thongden himself who met me at the door. "Nice to see you again," he said with unnecessary formality. And with a gesture, he invited me in, then led me through the empty waiting room to the examining room at the rear. As I followed behind him, I saw that he had exchanged the white coat with its white shirt and tie and business trousers for something more suitable, at least to my mind. He wore instead the long, brocaded Tibetan robe that I had seen on him when I'd visited his Manhattan brownstone last year. I had a strange feeling that we were getting back into familiar territory. He was becoming more like himself. He even looked more Oriental than on my last visit. And this time, even the examining room had changed. No longer did it have the balanced luminescence from the single wall panel. Instead, the room was shrouded in shadow except for a small glow of light around a large round mirror that sat in a frame before an armless padded chair. Immediately in front of the chair, on the wall, was a small panel inset with four colored buttons.

"What now?" I said, pausing and trying to peer through the dimness, the better to see him.

"Do please sit in the chair," he said, without any preliminaries. "And position yourself in front of the mirror."

I didn't move. I looked from the chair to the mirror and back to him. "I think you'd better explain first."

I managed to filter a reassuring smile from the darkness around his features. "That's exactly what this is," he promised. "An explanation, by demonstration. If you follow my instructions, it'll save a lot of needless questions later. You're not superstitious about mirrors, are you?"

"Not yet," I commented sardonically. But I gave in, settled myself onto the chair, and found myself gazing into the mirror. But the image that was reflected in it was so distorted I couldn't recognize myself. In fact, I couldn't have recognized any face in that grotesquerie of twisted features. "And what's that supposed to be?" I asked, feeling a twinge of nervousness.

"Nothing, nothing at all. Raw material for a face, you might say. It's up to you. The mirror surface," he went on, "is activated by four small motors that shift a number of hidden planes on the mirror up and down and side to side. Each of those four buttons controls a motor. Your task is to keep operating the buttons until the mirror produces a satisfactory reflection of your own face. Do you think you might like to try that?"

Without answering at first, I pressed the yellow button at the far left and saw the upper left quadrant of the mirror shift and cause a change in the reflection. "I see. Fun and games. Do I have to finish in any set amount of time?"

"No, take all the time you want. Just tell me when you've—found yourself." I caught a glimpse of a grin that was just a shade malevolent. Or perhaps it was a trick of the shadows. It was easy to imagine anything in that faintly lit room where the only clarity seemed to come from the mirror itself.

"Well, as soon as I get the hang of it, it shouldn't take long."

For a time, as I fiddled with the buttons, working at first with very light touches to effect the most minimal movement, I had a sense of Thongden standing behind me and watching. But it didn't take long before the shiftings of the mirror got so fascinating that I began to forget about everything else. In a few more minutes, I got comfortable using four fingers to shift the four buttons at the same time, and very soon I began to get the outlines of a normal face. Of course, it wasn't my face, but it seemed to me that a few touches here and there, a few changes to the jawline and the shape of the head, and I'd begin to get closer to what I really looked like. But somehow, my sense of time got thrown off. I became so fascinated with the problem of altering a segment here, readjusting a feature there, reshaping various parts to accord with a self-image that seemed to alter ever so slightly whenever I began to approximate my own remembered features, that I completely forgot about Thongden standing behind me and watching.

After a countless number of tries, I found myself observing images that were not only not myself, but increasingly demonic and hallucinatory—brutish creatures with pointed ears and narrow cranial portions, things that had hairy cheeks and long, double-lidded reptilian eyes. Finally, in a flicker of returning sanity I realized that I had been hallucinating, and the unnatural physiognomies were not in the mirror at all, but in my own head, conjured out of the fluttering shadows and the strained attention that kept my eyes fixed on that glowing mirror surface. But the mirror itself reflected only an ordinary male face of no particular character that was in no way recognizable as either myself or anyone I knew. I suddenly realized that a great deal of time had passed, and in a moment of panic, I turned and saw Thongden still standing watchfully behind me.

"You seem to be having some trouble," he said.

"It's not working right," I said. "It's fixed not to work right."

"Doesn't it respond exactly as you wish?"

I thought about that for a moment, then, without answering, began working the buttons again. Thongden was right, of course. The mirrors behaved exactly as I directed. But as I continued struggling to get a recognizable image of myself, I began to feel dizzy. This was followed by spasms of nausea. My stomach churned. It was like being seasick. As I tried one thing and then another in increasingly frenetic assaults on the buttons, I began to realize that I wasn't really sure what I looked like. Then came a feeling of panic. I turned abruptly from the mirror. It struck me then that this was what Thongden was trying to get me to understand. But even at that, I had this irrational seizure of anxiety about not having any reality at all. The fear prompted me to ask him suddenly, "Have you got a real mirror around here?"

"Why?"

"I—I think—I'm not—I mean I've lost touch with what I look like. If I could see myself in a real mirror for only a few seconds . . ."

"Aah," Thongden said. "And how would the mirror help?"

"It would give me a reference point," I responded with some irritation.

"It is strange, is it not," Thongden said, still standing there with his hands folded inside the sleeves of his robe, "that the mirror seems to know more than we do about ourselves?" He crossed the room and switched on the light, which left me temporarily blinded in the sudden full illumination. Then, as the room came into clear focus and I recognized it as the same examining room I had visited once before, I felt released from a kind of spell I felt I had put myself into. I got up from the seat facing the mirror and took the chair near his gray desk. "Is this a test you put all your patients through?" I asked.

"It was designed only for you," he explained to my surprise.

"For me? Why? All this trouble, to establish what?"

"I knew that you would be quick to understand."

"Apparently I wasn't."

"On the contrary. You are now fully aware that what we think we are is no more than a reflection in a mirror. So much so that, in fact, you cannot truly say that you look like either this or that or anything."

"Yes and no," I said grudgingly. "I have no trouble recognizing my wife, for example."

"No, no, you recognize the image of her you have created. I'm sure she sees herself quite differently. Come now, are you going to deny it just for the sake of argument?"

He folded his arms and thrust his hands into the sleeves of his robe. "You know, coming to terms with a mirror doesn't happen all at once. It starts early, in childhood. Children slowly strike up a deal with a mirror and agree to a certain way of seeing themselves. Then they still find it a little surprising to see themselves in profile and have to make a further adjustment for that. So what you see in the mirror is something you have decided on after much trial and error. It's all imagination. Have you not already learned how powerful the imagination is? This time, we will go further and allow you to discover that it is the chief organ of what we call consciousness. I think you might really like that."

I nodded, but in a careful tentative manner, acknowledging agreement, but still feeling that there was more to be said on the question. "And why," I asked, "have you decided to inflict this particular lesson on me at this time? What has it to do with my Bruce Wayne image and its associated financial problems?"

"Everything," Thongden replied unexpectedly. He had settled himself comfortably now on the floor, sitting in a relaxed lotus position as he watched me. "Also it has to do with the quid pro quo I mentioned to you. You can help us at the same time."

"Us?"

"Nelson Rimpoche and myself, on the personal level. More broadly, the people of Tibet."

"And how do I do that?"

"By assuming the most interesting of your unexpressed personalities. Even though you have never really acknowledged it, your Bruce Wayne phantasm is basically much more interesting than Superman. And far more complex."

"I'm afraid this is getting far away from me," I said.

"I am talking about the solution for your problem and ours," he insisted.

"My Bruce Wayne? How?"

"You must assume that personality. You will then see for yourself."

"But I'm not Bruce Wayne. How can I—?"

"As you just experienced, you're not really Alvin Schwartz either. But in fact, you created both. If you can assume your Alvin personality, it should be just as simple to take on the Bruce one."

"And how am I supposed to accomplish that?"

I had come to see Thongden on this particular day expecting some interesting revelations about myself. I had also, as I told Kay, been prepared for some special demands he would make on me in return, and about which I had some trepidation. But I hadn't an inkling about how far beyond my wildest expectations this meeting was to carry me.

Thongden now reminded me of something he had taught me last year: the art of transferring consciousness. "It's really not much different than changing into a different suit of clothes. The way I change my own costumes from time to time, as you must have noticed."

I remarked that he had certainly done an excellent crossover, from yesterday's modern psychotherapist, to—a *kuten*. I suddenly remembered the word as one he had taught me last year, meaning something like a kind of oracular medium, associated in Tibet with such important psychic institutions as the eighth-century Nechung oracle, still consulted on matters of state by the current Dalai Lama. On such occasions, the *kuten* is dressed in multilayered garments of which the outer one is an ornate silken robe decorated in designs of the four primary colors on a field of gold. In the one Thongden had worn during one of my visits to his Manhattan brownstone, there had been a highly polished steel circular mirror over his breast, the frame studded with clusters of turquoise and amethyst, on whose surface was inscribed the mantra of the protector divinity, Dorje Drakden, to be summoned by the *kuten*. But this time, Thongden's outfit lacked the mirror—which I now recognized in the enlarged version before which he had just had me sitting and trying to create my own reflection.

"So, yes," I acknowledged. "You even change your features in the process. So, what do you do? Snap your fingers three times, jump up and down and, presto, you've got a new consciousness? Sure beats the hell out of Superman's old phone booth." I realized, in making this comment, that I had grown so used to Thongden's mysterious tricks that I could treat them with a caustic casualness that best expressed both my interest and my bewilderment.

All this only produced a grin of satisfaction from Thongden. "You've got the right idea, but it's a little bit more complicated than that," he admitted. Then, with a wave of his arms, "But not for you, of course."

The problem, he told me, was "particularizing." How does a nonspecific personality, such as he had just shown me to be, become specific? Which was different from simply using exercises in *prajna* to shift from my Alvin consciousness into an ostrich or a bird or an old woman as I had once done. It was now more a matter of focusing the imagination from the awareness of having *no* identity into one of a particular identity, involving a powerful gathering of the imagination. "Imagination, you might say," and his grin widened as he said it, "is like the phone booth of consciousness. More seriously, it's the shaping aspect of being. Ontologically, you might say it's the way *being* assumes name and form, *nama rupa*."

"Great," I said, totally confused. "How do I do all that?"

"Well, instead of shifting from one consciousness into another, as you did in the past, you need to go another way."

"Why can't I just shift from my Alvin consciousness to my Bruce phantasm as I did with Superman?"

"For one thing, you were able to do that because you were confronted with a life and death situation when that carnival ride collapsed. You had to make the leap. But now you know that you would be leaping from nowhere. You know that your Alvin consciousness isn't real. Even though you might try to pretend otherwise. The fact is, you know. So instead, you must rely on your phone booth—your energy–imagination complex where you simply focus into your Bruce Wayne phantasm. You clothe yourself in that image, in other words."

"Just like that?"

"Do it," Thongden admonished. "At this moment, when you've lost your belief in your Alvin personality, you can do it on your own." He clapped his hands and shouted suddenly, "Go!"

I closed my eyes. I tried to think of myself as Bruce Wayne. For several long minutes, nothing happened. I opened my eyes again. "I'm wasting my time," I said.

Suddenly Thongden began laughing.

"What's so funny? I can't sit around here all day playing games. I've got things to do," I insisted, feeling as though I were suddenly imprisoned in a time-wasting and silly situation that was leading nowhere.

"Listen to yourself," Thongden said, his laughter diminishing into a wide grin as he studied me. "Since when did time get to be so important to you? Whose voice is that, anyway?" And he caught me by the arm and led me to the mirror, which he had somehow reset to normal. Then he swung me down onto the facing chair and told me to look at myself.

I stared at the reflection. "Who the hell is that?" I said. "It's not me."

"That depends," Thongden said. "Look more carefully. It's not Alvin, that's true. But, it's someone you know."

I stared again, noting the hard jawline, the somewhat furrowed brow, the well-chiseled lips pulled tight, one upon the other, in a tense, anticipatory manner.

"Damn," I exploded.

"Damn right," Thongden said, again on the verge of laughter. "You know yourself now, don't you?"

"Bruce Wayne," I muttered.

"About thirty-five years old. Successful, driven, and not very happy. You don't like yourself much, do you, Bruce?"

"What do you mean by that?" I demanded.

It was a strange situation. I really had assumed the Bruce Wayne personality as I had always envisioned it. But a part of me remained detached, watching as though from over my own shoulder. Perhaps, I seemed to think with that detached part of me, there remained with me not the Alvin personality so much as that other unformed reality that was neither this nor that, nameless and formless, inactive, but aware of what was going on, aware enough to realize that the Bruce personality made me extremely uncomfortable.

It seemed too driven, too angry, too fixated on deep feelings of self-righteousness and cold hard justice. It was precisely the way I used to think of Bruce Wayne when I was writing Batman for the comics. And it was why, though I did the job, I didn't find nearly the same relish in it that I did with Superman. By comparison, Superman had charm, he was more at peace with himself, and he pursued a more merciful image of justice than Bruce/Batman.

Not that any of these things were inherent in either of the characters per se. They were just comic strips. But the process of writing about them required the writer to clothe them with distinctive personalities. You have to believe in your characters to make them convincing; otherwise, your stories don't have any life. And obviously, the Bruce Wayne I created was a product of the way I interpreted Batman's origins, as first created by fellow writer, Bill Finger, who transformed the grotesque art of Bob Kane into the unique and strangely twisted Batman.

In brief, according to Finger, Bruce, as a child, saw his parents killed in cold blood during a robbery. The event so traumatized the young Bruce that he then and there decided to dedicate his life not only to finding his parents' killer, but to fighting crime everywhere. So, during the day, as Bruce Wayne he dedicated himself to building on the inheritance from his father by becoming a kind of financial wizard. This made it possible to cover the high financial costs of pursuing a night life as the crime-avenging and deadly Batman, complete with his costly Batcave, with its crime research lab, its anticrime weapons, and all its gimmicks, including those marvels of automotive and aerial technology, the Batmobile and the Batplane. Much of the rest of his time he spent in bodybuilding and the acquisition of advanced martial arts techniques. The little time he had left over for any kind of personal or social life he tended to use by assuming the role of a playboy socialite, the better to cover up his dedicated life as crime fighter.

That was the comic strip character as it was given to me by Finger, who preceded me at DC Comics. To write such a character, I had to feel and put myself into the driven qualities of a secret vigilante lifestyle with which I personally felt little affinity. And at this moment, standing there in Thongden's examining room and feeling what it was actually like to *be* the Bruce Wayne my imagination had created under Bill's guidance, I could again feel the harsh, driven, fixated quality of that personality. I could also begin to understand why, as Alvin, I had functioned so poorly in financial matters—as a kind of overreaction to that Bruce personality. It wasn't the entire story, I suspected, but it was a part of it.

I was able to feel all of those things from an exterior vantage point as I stood there in Thongden's studio. And though I grasped quite well by now that I had shifted my active awareness into a kind of *tulpa* of Bruce Wayne, I was powerless to influence it. As Bruce, I had to act like Bruce.

However, there was still something essential missing. There was no Batman. I had been shifted with Thongden's support into my Bruce Wayne phantasm. But I really had no desire to go whole hog with this and also turn myself into Batman.

Except for one very important thing. It took only five minutes of experiencing what it was like to be Bruce Wayne before I realized that if I didn't go ahead and take on the whole Batman personality as well, I'd have no way to get rid of the terrible pent-up anger, the boiling, volatile pressures that drove Bruce Wayne. Without Batman, my anger would burst out in cruelty and sadism and a kind of murderous rage that would destroy my abilities to play my financial role and might, in the end, even destroy my life. And somehow, I knew also that Thongden had put me into this personality for a purpose of his own, and I couldn't easily get out of it, until that purpose had been realized. I turned on Thongden and told him bluntly what I'd been thinking and feeling.

"You're absolutely right," Thongden said, after hearing me out. "You'll have to create your Batman from scratch, just as the comic strip version of Bruce Wayne did. Except that you can escape the years of training. You already have the necessary fitness built in, uh, Bruce."

As I listened to him saying that, and addressing me familiarly as Bruce, my new personality took over. I had to struggle against an impulse to grab him by the front of that ornate robe of his, lift him from his feet, and shake him like a puppy. As these thoughts surged through me, he fixed his full, lambent gaze on me and shook his head. "Don't waste your energy misdirecting your anger," he warned. "Also, remember that you're here to get rid of all that wasted aggression. Through your Batman persona. Only, not right away."

"What's that supposed to mean?" I demanded, just barely mollified. But I knew I had to keep my anger under control.

"It means that first, Nelson Rimpoche and I need your help. More particularly, we need the help of the Batman you're going to create."

"Remember," I (Bruce) reminded him, "you get no help from Batman unless there's serious crime involved. You know very well, he's conditioned that way, for my own self-protection. To keep my anger within acceptable bounds. I mean, there'd be no point in Batman's existence otherwise."

"I understand," Thongden agreed. "But you can be sure, there's a very serious crime involved."

"Yes?"

"The Chinese destruction of the Tibetan people. Also, a murder that's being planned at this very moment."

"Whose murder?"

Thongden raised his head and gazed soberly at me. "Mine," he said.

Chapter Four

By the time I finally, eventually, got back home again and saw Kay, I felt as though I hadn't seen her in years. Because in fact, I had been set on a four-year time track by Thongden. But I couldn't have actually been away more than two months. At least, I thought it must have been about two months—until Kay, somewhat startled at the fervor with which I hugged her when she first opened the door for me, said, "What is it? You act as if you haven't seen me for ages."

I released her, noting how strange she seemed to me. "It did seem like ages, even though it was only, well, a couple of months."

She gave me one of her incomprehensible looks, took me by the hand, and led me to the couch. She made me sit down. She rested a cool palm on my forehead, probing for fever. "You seem normal enough. What's this about two months?"

I shrugged. "Give or take a few days. How long was I gone then?"

"Two days."

"What?"

"Two days," she repeated. "Why would I make it up?"

I sat forward on the couch, rested my elbows on my knees and cupped my chin in my hands while I stared at the floor, trying to pull my thoughts together.

"Would you like to tell me about it now?" I heard Kay saying. "Or would you rather have something to eat first?"

I shook my head. "I just ate," I said.

"Oh? Where?"

I looked at her and realized, even as I answered, that something had gotten very mixed up. "Buckingham Palace," I said.

"You mean, in Britain," she said finally, not asking it as a question, merely setting the location. When she put it that way, I knew she believed me, but she was going to require an explanation. We'd been through things like this before, ever since Thongden had come into our lives.

He insisted that I take my Bruce Wayne personality out for a trial run that very day, I explained to Kay. This was after I had told her about the experiments with the mirrors, and other methods he'd used to break down my identification with my Alvin Schwartz personality.

"It's almost like what you call bar hopping, except that you go from personality to personality," Thongden said. "And you don't need cabs either," he added with that portentous grin he used to beam at me. "Just a few breaths and you're off and away."

And then he had me go through that leap from being non-Alvin to being Bruce again, until I was standing in front of him in that funny blue suit and, as a real mirror showed me, that collar-ad face.

"Now, go out and test out your new identity," he ordered.

"What do you mean, test it out?"

"Go outside. Go anywhere you like where you'll feel comfortable. And just be the Bruce Wayne you've always imagined."

But I knew I couldn't just be that. It was a little more complicated. Because there was something, some bedrock of ultimate self, I suspect, that seemed to stand outside the whole thing, watching it. I tried to tell Thongden that, but the words didn't come out, because I couldn't speak out of that ultimate self. I had to make myself say it through Bruce Wayne, and they weren't quite the words I meant to use.

"Someone's watching me," Bruce said. Or rather, I said it, speaking as Bruce.

"Of course," Thongden acknowledged. "Living beings always tend to watch themselves. It's what we call self-consciousness. Something you haven't ever experienced directly, Bruce. But you'll learn it and be happy for it."

"Like acquiring a conscience, you mean?" Bruce said.

Thongden shrugged. "Something like that."

"I haven't much use for a conscience," Bruce announced, in the kind of tight-lipped, two-dimensional manner that represented his personality in my eyes.

"Hmm. We'll see, won't we?" Thongden said. But he looked troubled for the first time. "Anyway, this is a trial run. Go somewhere. Spend the day. See how you handle yourself. A lot will be depending on you."

And that was when my Bruce Wayne phantasm simply walked out. I found my car—that is, Alvin's car—standing in the driveway, got in it, backed out and onto 520 East, and headed for Merritt Island, and home. That is, I thought I was heading home. But I didn't get there. Somehow, I found myself in the Winn-Dixie shopping center in Cocoa Beach, about four miles east of our condo. And that was where the whole thing began to come apart. My memory is not very clear on all the little in-between steps until I found myself standing on the pavement alongside an astonished group of spectators, while we watched this monstrous creature that looked like Batman pursue a couple of would-be holdup men. I think they'd just come out of the Radio Shack right next to the Winn-Dixie supermarket when I had this sense of shucking my Bruce Wayne getup. I don't know how I did it, but I went for that bedraggled and luckless pair, cornered them in an alley, and beat them with a brutal relish that left the silent watching part of me sick to my stomach. Somehow, I had fragmented into two totally different personalities. Thongden's bad mix simply hadn't worked from the outset.

Next thing I remember, I told Kay, was driving again. There was no Bruce, no Batman, only myself with this sick, foggy feeling that I had to get back to Thongden's place as soon as I could before any further fragmentation destroyed what I had begun to think of once more as the real me, Alvin.

"I made a mistake," Thongden had said. "The Wayne personality won't hold. It's too alien to you." He looked concerned and somewhat lachrymose as he sat there, still in his *kuten* robe. His gaze traveled to the ceiling. "Somewhere," he pondered as though conducting a colloquy with himself, "there must be a financial influence that caused you to get involved in the first place, even if unsuccessfully."

"The only such influence I can remember," I announced suddenly, a little surprised at the aptness of the memory, "was my mother."

"Yes?"

I shrugged. "She had an inordinate desire for me to become rich. She used to play the market herself in a small way, usually with disastrous results."

"Like mother like son," Thongden said.

"Not exactly. She really didn't know what she was doing. She'd get tips from people and invest impulsively. She never even understood how the market worked."

"But you do?"

"I not only do, in spite of recent results, I really feel I have a gift for it. I don't know what it is, but if I didn't have to persuade my wife, I'm sure I could turn these recent losses around. In fact, I'm convinced. Which is why, when I think about it, I have to ask myself again: What am I doing here?"

"You're here out of my need," Thongden reminded me in very

grave tones. "But what you've just said may be very revealing."

"In what way?"

"Your conviction about your financial ability suggests another possibility."

"What do you mean?"

"A bleedthrough."

"What?"

Thongden shrugged. "Without getting into a lot of complex explanations, it has something to do with reincarnation."

"You mean, in one of my previous lives, I was John D. Rockefeller or something? Hmm, of course, not Rockefeller exactly. He was still alive when I was a kid."

"You must forget your fixation on linear time. In reality, as I've explained to you before, everything is happening at once. You don't have any previous lives. But everyone has literally dozens of simultaneous selves."

"You mean, maybe even Rockefeller?"

"Not too likely. He had none of your gentleness. But there must be some bleedthrough from someone, to convince you that you can make a success of the stock market. It's like this," Thongden explained. "Have you ever seen someone with a special talent, like playing the piano? Someone who never even had lessons, but seems to have what we like to call an obvious talent?"

"Well, sure. In fact, I hate to bring up my mother again, but she was really good on the piano. Good enough to play in the old silent-movie houses. And she was virtually self-taught."

Thongden nodded. "Very likely a bleedthrough. A direct influence from one of her alternate selves."

"She was very fond of Liszt. Do you think—?"

Thongden gave a characteristic shrug. "Who can say?"

"But you're suggesting I have an alternate self who's a financial expert? That's where I'm getting it from?"

"It would be worth exploring," Thongden said.

"And how would we do that? Another one of your special tricks?"

"You give me too much credit. It's done every day. Surely you know about hypnotic regression?"

"I never took it too seriously. Bridey Murphy? Stuff like that?"

Thongden nodded. "Mostly, it's a crude method because the hypnotists don't really know what they're looking for. So the so-called past personalities are just pulled out of a grab-bag of possibilities. We have the advantage of knowing what we're looking for."

"A financier."

"Yes, but reasonably contemporary. A kind of parallel self."

"What if I don't have such a parallel self?"

Thongden raised his hands in a gesture of resignation. "Then we only have Bruce Wayne. Not a viable prospect. But, that drive of yours, that certainty, it must be coming from somewhere. And from someone of whom Bruce Wayne is just a negative caricature. We should at least try."

Chapter Five

Kay interrupted my narration at this point. She held up her hand to silence me, got off the couch and walked out to the screened patio through the sliding glass door. I stood back, watching her, wondering. After some moments of staring at her back, I joined her on the patio.

"Something's bothering you," I said.

She turned to face me, offering a mute nod in response.

"Tell me," I pleaded.

Her upper lip descended over her lower one for a moment. "I was waiting here for two days," she said. "But as you talk, I see more and more that you really were away . . . oh my God, was it really four years?" She repeated the question, "Four years?"

I nodded with a confessional sort of awkwardness.

"During that four years, when I was out of your life," she added tremulously, "there was someone else? There had to be."

I nodded again, but added, "It wasn't my life. It wasn't me, Alvin. I was there in a way, but only the way a dream is there, a lurking awareness of being more than the life I was living."

"I could feel the distance when you were talking before."

"Distance?" I repeated.

"You look at me with such searching expressions. I—I feel the unfamiliarity that four years must have put between us. Not for me. But for you."

I stepped back, looked away, and sighed. "Being here is like stepping into the reality of a recurring dream. I'm getting back, by degrees, that's true. And I mean, there was always a bleedthrough during those years. A very strong one. So, in a way, you were always present. But only at intervals. I'm not even quite used to myself yet." I stood close beside her now and put a hand on her arm. "You know, I want to be back. Although I'll always be aware that we're all much more than we know."

She reached up and put her hands on my shoulders. "Are you glad to be back? Does it matter? I mean—" She shook her head quickly. It was almost a shudder. I could see the glisten of tears in her eyes. "—is this where you prefer to be?"

"Yes," I said, knowing it was the only thing I could say. I could not admit to her I was also sorry to have left the other life. But perhaps, in telling her about it, I could bring her into it with me. I took her by the arm and led her back into the living room.

"Did he hypnotize you? Is that how he did it?"

No, I told her, he helped me through his breathing techniques. Somehow, he seemed able to enter that same state with me. All through it, I could feel him alongside me. After a time, when I became aware of the room again and the sound of his voice, I also remembered images of another life. And a strange name that I couldn't pronounce. I asked him what had happened.

"We found your parallel self," Thongden said. "The financier."

"With a strange name?"

"I suppose you could call it strange. The name was Bazenrüd. Hungarian, actually."

"And this Bazenrüd, is me?"

"Not exactly."

"Then—?"

"If you try to think of this other personality along a time track, as someone you might have been in the past, then you'd have no trouble understanding what a reincarnational personality is? Am I correct?"

"I suppose so. Somebody I once was, but not me. Although talents acquired in an earlier life can sometimes show echoes in my present one. Right?"

"That's the commonly accepted notion. Except that in reality, all these so-called past lives—and you'll have to include future lives as well—are all going on at once."

I nodded. "A little hard to grasp, but—" And then a sudden irruption of memory trapped my attention. "—Bazenrüd, I remember that name now. There was an article I picked up in a magazine at the dentist's, maybe ten, twelve years ago. Way back. But as I recall it, wasn't this fellow sort of a shady arms dealer? Very wealthy? Very secretive? Very powerful? Lived a kind of mysterious underground life?" I grew excited, my voice rising a little higher with each burst of returning memory.

"Mostly correct. Except for the arms dealer part. What he was, or is, is a financier. Never dealt in arms at all. By getting to know him, you might be able to do a better job dealing with your own finances."

"How do I do that? And where do your plans come into it? I'm not forgetting that part of it."

"So many questions," Thongden said. "But you don't really have to do anything."

"About becoming Bazenrüd?"

"No, I meant about my problem. It will happen by itself."

"There's someone out to get rid of you, you tell me, and you send me back there, and then you say I don't have to do anything? How do I even find this would-be assassin?"

"It will happen," Thongden said. "It's not a thing like knowledge. It has more to do with the way events are constructed. There's the aspect of grace, and there's the dark side. A kind of split series of space–time events. You and I are obviously here for the purpose of uniting a specific group of space–time events. It is why we have crossed at this point, and why you have drawn this particular timeline. You are here to help me. Through your own financial problem."

He paused, studied me for a moment as though to see how well all this was going down, then proceeded. "Every possible outcome can occur. The one you experienced thirteen years from now does not disappear, because you have created the timeline that connects it to this present. But it's no more real than the one you can help us create now. All planes of being are possible. Without affecting the plane you find yourself on in this moment, you can still help bring about that other possibility."

Now he had really lost me. "What other possibility?" I asked.

Thongden had me sit in the big chair facing his desk. He brought his face close to mine as though through some force of his own being he could help me digest what he was saying. "In the multilayered universe, as it really exists," he explained carefully, "there are clumps of events that belong together, that are related in a kind of noncausal grouping, their connection having to do with value and meaning rather than material events. And that is why, if you pursue your own financial goals, you will bring everything else along with you."

"You're sure of that?" I said.

"Of course not. I'm not omniscient."

"Then why . . ."

"Because if you don't do it," he said, "you'll wind up a pauper in your final years. That's guaranteed."

"And you'll be dead?"

"Death cannot be in my experience. But I can certainly be dissolved."

"That's what they're working on?"

"According to Nelson Rimpoche."

"So our only choice, then, is Bazenrüd?"

"Which, even though it's not guaranteed, is a better choice than doing nothing. Wouldn't you agree?" he finished, fixing me with his familiar craggy smile.

He started me on my way with his customary technique of *nadi-sudi*. I felt it going on, and on, for a long time. Until . . . there I was, sitting in a familiar chair, looking out a familiar window. And exactly the way we always presume a personal history in dreams, I knew exactly who I was, how I had gotten where I was, what I was doing at that moment. I was not Alvin Schwartz. But I wasn't Bazenrüd either. My name was Edward Horgan, and I had never heard of anyone named Bazenrüd.

Chapter Six

"Edward Horgan?" Kay repeated. "That's not what you were expecting, was it?"

"It wasn't what Alvin Schwartz was expecting. But in that situation, *I* wasn't expecting anything other than being what I was. Which was a man in his mid-forties, an American, with a grown son going to engineering school in the United States while I continued my business activities in Switzerland as a broker, primarily in chemical products. My wife had died many years ago. That was quite a distinct memory. And while my son was growing up, I had worked as a purchasing agent for Dupont. Then I had branched out on my own, buying and selling commodities for chemical companies. After some years, I got to know where many things were to be found that were in short supply. Not just chemical products and raw materials. I developed sources of information that put me way ahead of the game. Since I was operating in an international market, I found it worth my while to open an office in Geneva, Switzerland. It was the beginning of the eighties, and you might say I was doing nicely. Nothing spectacular but nicely."

"It all sounds so very nice and boring," Kay said. "And Bazenrüd, what happened to him? Where was the great financier? What had Thongden gotten you into?"

It was hard to answer her at first. I knew this was going to be the most difficult part of the whole narration. Not only because I had to recall it, piece by piece from a kind of parallel memory, but because I now had to tell Kay about Lorraine.

I managed, first, to assure her that she could stop thinking about Horgan as me, that is, as Alvin. He was a parallel self, yes. But basically, a different individual with whom I shared what Thongden always described as significant bleedthroughs. So then I told her about the French film star, Lorraine. I told her how, in the experience of the orderly and essentially conventional businessman that I, Edward Horgan, was, Lorraine was completely unlike any woman I had ever met.

As soon as I began to speak of it, I felt drawn into it once more, as though I were reliving yesterday. I got onto this thing about the movies first. And then I talked to Kay more out of a sense of being Edward Horgan. It was easier that way, easier to say things that, if they seemed to come from me, as Alvin, might be painful for her.

Not being a moviegoer, I proceeded to explain to her, I—that is, Edward Horgan—had never especially developed any interest in movies. So I had never seen any of Lorraine's films, although when I met her she was making her twenty-first. As I was soon to learn, she only used that single name, Lorraine. She'd had it legalized, used it to sign contracts and conduct all her other business. No one at any of the studios actually knew her real last name, although she had told the publicity people that her family name was Chalifoux, which, if you translate it from the way it sounds, means Crazy Cat. That was why she dropped it, she said to the public. None of it was true. Her real name was Bazenrüd, a fact soon to become known only to me, Edward Horgan, and later on, a few others.

At the time we met, Lorraine was under contract with a British studio filming in Switzerland, not far from Geneva where my offices were located. It was she who initiated our meeting.

It was a cool spring morning. My office was located in a building about six blocks northeast of Parc Villa Barton. From my office window, I looked out across Lake Geneva and could see early signs of spring, brighter patches of green forming within the darker greens of the conifers growing on the slopes north of the city. It was that remarkably clear a day. My secretary was out of the office on a minor errand when the phone rang, so I took the call myself. I heard a woman's voice on the other end of the line, a lovely, precise voice, very musical and very controlled. She asked if I was Edward Horgan, and when I told her I was, she said, "I am Lorraine. I would like to see you on a matter of business."

"Lorraine who?" I asked.

"Just Lorraine." This reply was followed by a sighing sound of light laughter. "*The* Lorraine."

"I'm sorry," I said, "I'm afraid I don't understand."

"Lorraine, the actress. Surely you go to the cinema from time to time?"

"Actually, very rarely." And then it dawned on me. Of course I had heard the name. Lorraine was quite well known, even to non-moviegoers like me. I said, rather idiotically, "You mean, Lorraine, the movie actress? You're Lorraine?" Again that sighing sound with its mild echo of laughter.

"Do you know any other?" she asked.

I was certain that someone was having a little joke at my expense. I tried to relate that voice to some of the women I had met or seen recently. But I drew a blank. I couldn't think of any male friends who'd be likely to set up something like this, although quite a few of them had told me I ought to circulate more. Nevertheless, I played it carefully. "Are you sure it's Edward Horgan you want?"

"You are Edward Horgan, the American chemist and commodities consultant?"

"Yes, I am."

"Then I would be grateful if you could find time to meet with me. At your earliest convenience."

"I see. Yes. But what about?" I was still doubtful she was who she claimed to be.

"A matter of business," she told me. "Commodities business."

"Really?" It was surprise that made me hesitate, but not for long. "You have some interest in the commodities business, then, Miss Lorraine?"

"In both the business and in you, Mr. Horgan."

With that reply, I was convinced that someone was putting me on. But there was a fascinating quality in her voice. I was curious. Besides, things were rather slow at the office on that particular morning. I responded impulsively. "How soon can you get here?"

"I'll be there in twenty minutes, Mr. Horgan. Thank you." And she hung up.

She arrived exactly on time. My secretary was still out, and Lorraine came directly into my office, taking rather long strides for a small woman, holding out her hand to which I touched my lips. She wore a very conservative, rather tailored suit. She was, as far as I could tell, without makeup except for a trace of lipstick, and she didn't look a lot like the actress I had seen in so many photos and billboards. Her pale blonde hair was worn rather short, not mannishly short, but not quite falling to her shoulders. And her features, apparently without enhancement of any kind, were both diminutive and so precisely formed that they almost went beyond the bounds of the three-dimensional. Rather like, to use a strange but accurate metaphor, something viewed in ultrahigh resolution. More penetrating than striking, more presence than appearance. For a moment, I thought she might not be Lorraine, after all. She seemed so much less and, at the same time, so much more than her public image. But there was no mistaking the trained gestures, the walk, the way she settled into the chair I offered her. If these were not the mannerisms of a trained actress, then they reflected the schooling of a lady. The word *princess* actually formed in my mind. And my hand shook slightly as I reached over to light her cigarette. She inhaled slowly, then released a thin tendril of smoke as she gave me an odd mischievous smile.

"You will have to learn to be more comfortable with me, since we're going to be partners."

"I see," I said to her, feeling my face reddening at her brashness. But of course, I didn't see. "Does this have to do with some kind of movie you intend to make?"

Again I heard that diluted little laugh of hers as she watched me through a filament of cigarette smoke. "I hope never to have to make another film," she declared. "And with your help, I never shall." Now she brought the cigarette down, pressed it out deliberately in the ashtray I had placed at a corner of my desk, and leaned toward me.

"For a really gifted performer, the cinema is a very small, very provincial kind of stage. I have outgrown it. I have—what shall I say?—other interests. There are much larger stages than the cinema or the theater can offer."

"Like Ronald Reagan, the actor, becoming president of the United States?" I offered, somewhat dryly, thinking perhaps she had political ambitions.

She shook her head. "Mr. Reagan?" She repeated the head shake. "He never left the cinema. Instead he turned the whole country into a movie lot. More interesting is the simple fact that an actor became president of the United States, don't you think? And," she added pointedly, "that another actor became Pope."

I admitted to her that a performance full of style seemed to enjoy an advantage over substance in many areas of public activity. But it still wasn't clear whether she aspired to something like the presidency of France. The conversation was getting stranger and stranger as she then proceeded to say, "But these days the best performances take place out of the limelight, on smaller, more particularized stages. The mass audience is not nearly so interesting as smaller, more specialized audiences, the transnational corporation, for example. That is why I have come to you, a man with broad entrée to that stage."

I had no idea what she was getting at, or what she meant by performing on the stage of what she called the transnational corporation. But she seemed so certain of herself, I was impressed. More than that, I was transfixed. Looking into her eyes as she spoke, I could easily have spent the morning doing only that. So I simply nodded agreement, encouraging her to continue.

She held her hands out in front of her, locked her fingers together and then shook them in my direction, an odd gesture, but one that turned out to be characteristic. "You are listening to me, but like a voyeur. Paying no real attention to what I am saying. If I did not know you better, I would leave right now."

Those words startled me right out of my fixation. "Know me better? And just how well do you know me?" I asked. "Maybe we'd better begin with that."

She smiled suddenly. "Ah, now you are listening. I know you well, Mr. Horgan. I have had you checked out, investigated, researched, I have even had you followed for some time. Does that shock you?"

"Oh no, not shocked. Just flabbergasted."

"Flabbergas—what is that word? An American expression?" She was frowning as she asked the question. Although she spoke very good English, her usage was rather stilted and overly proper. I told her that *flabbergasted* was a widely used term for being confounded, astonished, amazed. Why, I demanded, had I been targeted for these intrusive attentions of hers?

"One of the things I learned about you," she said, "is that you have a good head for monetary matters. That you're considered a monetary expert."

Now it was my turn to be amused. "I am considered something

of an expert," I admitted, "but on the other hand, I'd be hard put to tell you exactly what a monetary expert is. You see, there's never really been any agreement on whether monetary conditions influence the economy, or simply respond to the economy. And for two hundred years, the men who argued over this question were considered experts. In that sense, I'm also an expert. I don't know the answer either."

She responded with a laugh. "I have also heard that you were a man not weighed down with self-importance. A great advantage for our purposes. As for the monetary question, I am the only true expert," she asserted without a trace of modesty. "Does economic change originate with central banks which can deliberately increase the supply of money? Or does it begin with production and prices which raise the demand for loans, thereby increasing the money supply? That is the big question no one can agree on, yes?"

"Yes," I said. "So far, you're also an expert."

"The answer is, neither."

And then, to my surprise, she launched into a discussion of what had not as yet become very widely accepted at that time: the significance of the information age. The sum of her views was that all value was increasingly being shifted into information and the means of manipulating information. A lot of forward-thinking people were already expressing such views, but she herself, perhaps because of her theatrical experience, was of the opinion that information by itself was like gold ore. It needed refining and processing. And because of its nature, that could only be provided by what she archly referred to as "a sponsoring personality."

"With the right sponsor," she finished, "information becomes many times more valuable than in its unprocessed state. Like ore," she finished, smiling brightly.

Her remarks left me confused but still intrigued. I felt rather than understood that she was about to make an important point, something I hadn't really heard before. I asked her to explain further.

"You asked me before, why my 'intrusive attentions', as you called them, had been focused on you. The answer, Mr. Horgan, is the fact that your business functions only because you are a major source of information for your corporate clients. Information, Mr. Horgan, on where important commodities are to be found. You have spent many years acquiring that information. Your corporate clients are very dependent on you because their own businesses rest on the sort of information you supply. You do not get paid nearly well enough, from what I can see."

She was right about that, I realized, regardless of her economic theories.

"You know a great deal more," she added, "than you give yourself credit for. But you need someone to manage that information you possess, someone who knows how to put, as they say, the proper highlights on it, so as to get its maximum value in the marketplace."

By this point, she sounded absolutely mad to me. And while I wasn't convinced, I was so enthralled by her performance, that I continued to sit and listen as she went on in great detail about the role of information. It turned out finally that what she was urging me to accept is that economic behavior is entirely information driven, even before the so-called market begins to take over. And what she was proposing was to use my own highly credible background as a base, and from it, by means best known to her, reshape me into a processor and refiner of information in a way I had never dreamed of. But why? What was her real purpose?

I sensed something else behind her words, something far grander, far more daring and, in the deepest sense, far more necessary. Without her saying it directly, I could not avoid the feeling that she might have been preparing against something, some menace that she recognized in some deeply instinctive, or, more accurately, prophetic way. As yet she probably lacked the words for it, but its nature was such as to make all her other activities and concerns secondary. In a certain way, as I was to discover, like all great actresses, she was a *sensitif*. She was aware of things for which mere words lacked credibility. But what she knew or sensed, I had no clear idea, and I'm not sure that she did either.

But I did know in some way that her behavior was in response to a call, something that required her to start amassing her forces, to be prepared. How did I know this? Logically, I could only say that the lengths to which this absolutely sane but determined woman was prepared to go, so far as I could see, presaged just that. Perhaps I had some inkling of what might be coming myself, possibly from some aspect of my being that was beyond time, some aspect that was more than my empirical self. Did it make sense? Just barely. I don't think that any great moves, by anyone, were ever made for any other reason, as though within each of us there is imbedded a connection with everyone else, as well as with our own human past and future. Perhaps this was only grandiose speculation, but I can think of no better reason for my having allowed myself to be so influenced by her.

But at the moment, she had only her strong presentiment that business was the ground stage for some sort of coming struggle. I myself had already considered, during rare moments of inner candor, the discomfiting notion that wealth was being centralized in vast clots of power without any true human purpose. In the end, that was sure to bring strife and chaos and disaster. Most of the time, however, I didn't dwell on such morbidities. It wouldn't happen tomorrow. There was plenty of time for a more positive turn of events to annul such dire possibilities. Perhaps Lorraine had a greater sense of urgency, although I had no way as yet of being sure of that. Even though she tried to tell me. And she also was about to let me know that she was not going to let trivialities of local morality stand in the way.

I began, as I always do, with concrete facts. I questioned her about the true source of her inside knowledge, and demanded more detail about what she meant by "processing" information to open a way onto the transnational corporate stage.

Much to my embarrassment, Lorraine was very frank in her reply. "I am a leading cinema star, Mr. Horgan," she told me. "And among the stages on which I am called upon to perform is the bedroom. Do you suppose there are really enough foolish investors who would put their money into most of the films produced today, without some encouragement? And would you really be surprised to learn how many boardroom secrets are also revealed in the bedroom?"

"I suppose not," I said, wondering whether the warm flush I could feel on my face was visible to her. But she simply went on with her explanation.

"And so I learned what so many women like me, oh yes, men too, probably failed to notice, that the great mover of men and institutions is information. No major trader in the stock market makes a move without information. Research is an important source, but even better and more reliable is insider information, something that the absurd little laws of your country send people to prison for—oh, perhaps about one-half of one percent, men who for the most part are too indiscreet and too public in their activities. And better still is my kind of 'processed' information. Because for the first time, I will be applying a new kind of knowledge to the field, the knowledge of the performer. Also, my way will be very hidden."

"I don't understand what you mean by *hidden*."

"I am coming to that," she promised. "But perhaps we should go more slowly, Mr. Horgan. I have much to reveal to you. There are many dimensions beyond the three you are already familiar with." And that was when I asked her whether she had really acquired all this knowledge through her bedroom–boardroom activities. To which she replied, "Mostly." At that point, I couldn't resist asking her how she happened to be so singularly different from her colleagues in observing and putting together all this remarkable material. She seemed to have her answers already prepared.

She said that, for one thing, most performers who've achieved stardom are very happy to be where they are. There were some exceptions who, like herself, felt uncomfortable in the cinema. She detested being a public idol. She chafed at the restrictions of being part of the whole childish system. And yes, even at the bedroom requirements. Not for moral reasons. "Do you know," she said, "that economics was a subject in which I excelled when I attended university? Only for two years, mind you. But I felt that money and business activity were the real motive power of our civilization. Not the arts, not culture, not religion." She told me those were merely what she called "epiphenomena."

I disagreed with her. I told her that everything about my business— the location, manipulation, and sale of commodities—was ultimately based on one prime mover that was political, not economic. The Cold War, I assured her, was the operational factor behind everything.

"No," she insisted. "Corporate power will really assume center stage as a result of the end of the Cold War. Until that end comes, everything that troubles me is being held in suspension. I could almost hope the Cold War never ends." At this, I merely smiled indulgently at her.

"You do not see, as I do," she insisted, "the coming collapse of the Soviet Union."

"And how do you know that?" I asked, still indulgent.

"Because I understand economics. And economically, the Soviet Union is *sans faisibilité*, unfeasible."

It was a large statement. But there was something about the way she said it, as though she *knew*, that caused me to withhold further comment.

"But the problem is more than simple economics," she added. "It is because the Soviet information system is frozen, clogged completely in one direction, from the top down. That way, it will not last very long."

What could I have said in the face of such blatant certainty? "But your goal," I insisted. "It wouldn't just be money then. I'm not clear exactly where you're going."

"Not just money, no."

"Then what?"

That was when she began talking to me about her greatest teacher. One of her boardroom friends, in fact. An older man, since passed on. One of the things he taught her was that we never had to passively accept what life presented us with. If we desired something better, it was ours for the taking. With one condition. "It is not necessary to know precisely what the goal is," he had explained to her. "Goals never fully reveal themselves until you begin to take steps toward whatever vague goal outlines you do have." But it was necessary to begin moving toward it right away, he had insisted. "Waste no time in wishing or hoping. Start doing whatever your situation offers toward the achievement of your goal." That was his ultimate requirement. For Lorraine, that meant bringing together in some way her talents as a performer and her interests in economics. Plus her deeper instinct as a *sensitif* that there were problems developing in the world that only some countervailing power could cope with. "So I cannot say if it is money alone. Perhaps, yes, perhaps it will take much money." In any event, as she explained, the requirement to "begin with what she had," had demanded, to start with, even more boardroom-in-the-bedroom activity, where she could listen and learn. It was through being completely focused on that need that she began to realize how important the role of information was.

Suddenly, she stopped talking and searched me with an expression I couldn't quite fathom. I decided later that it was a bit of deliberate *mysterioso*, part of her arsenal, and that she'd trotted it out for effect. And then, in the next breath, she proposed that I take her to dinner so she could go about the business of educating me in a more leisurely fashion. I agreed.

In the end, she took me to dinner. We wound up on a side street I'd never visited before, in a small family-run restaurant that I'd never discovered in all my years in Geneva. I have a vague memory of very good food, but what I recall principally was the three hours we spent talking. Since I was the pupil, I did most of the listening.

It's admittedly a very strange story, but it gets stranger still. Because one might well ask, how does a man like myself, Edward Horgan, conservative by nature, reasonably comfortable with the way his life has been going, let himself get drawn into an undertaking that flies in the face of reality, common values, and appropriate behavior?

The simple answer is that she convinced me more by what she secretly believed than by what she said. She spoke to that part of me that somehow sensed the same possible future that she too sensed. And in the course of it, she managed to expose the false assumptions behind my notions of propriety, my conventional view of how the world operated, and my rather restricting economic orthodoxies.

Then she came to the really unusual part, the role of the performer. With all my knowledge of where and how to find metals and unprocessed materials, I was only at the beginning of the possible. What I didn't yet have but which she would help me set up was an organization whose purpose was getting information—using computers, spies, bribes, statisticians, psychological analyses, the whole congeries of what it takes to gather information. But, much more than that, an organization that provided a stage to lend credibility to the whole show.

At first I protested. I couldn't accept the use of spies and bribery, and said so in very clear terms. I talked about the error of trying to achieve worthwhile ends with tainted means. And she laughed, reminding me that I was behaving like the American auto manufacturers who, because of their management style, were blind to certain kinds of information about the changing nature of the market. What really persuaded me was the realization, as she pointed out, that I had indeed been aware of the bribery, the spying, the insider-trading operations of most of the big corporations I served, but I had deliberately blinded myself to it all. It was as though once I let go and allowed myself to accept it, I would be dropping over some kind of cliff of moral relativism where I'd be lost. After that, where was decency, honesty, self-respect, and all the other homely virtues that had been inculcated into me as a good middle-class American? But Lorraine pushed me over the cliff. In spite of her history, in spite of her questionable values, she clearly had enough moral clarity and self-respect for both of us.

And finally, there was the clincher, the totally childish, wild game of pretend—I can think of no other name for it—that she laid out for me. It awakened a long dormant, boyish love of adventure, of play, of sheer fun and excitement, along with that secret sense we both shared of saving the world from some as yet unformed future threat. I didn't realize how boring my life had become until she proposed it. I went for it, as they say, hook, line, and sinker.

Thinking as Edward, I now proceeded to explain for Kay's benefit that Lorraine hadn't chosen me out of the blue for this role, and it was literally a role, a grand performance. She had searched long and hard for someone who matched her specifications. She had spent thousands of dollars on information about likely prospects. To begin with, she needed someone who knew his way around the big corporations, who was trusted by them and who did his job in an area of business consulting that depended on good, solid information. At first, she had looked within the corporations for such an individual, but had gradually realized that she needed someone with a foot in the door of many different companies, an outside consultant. She also needed someone who would be relatively footloose, not tied down with family. Someone who was even rather solitary and not in the habit of keeping up much of a social life. And finally, she needed someone not too young, but young enough and personable enough to be a man with whom she could share a real rapport. I had been one among perhaps twenty different candidates she had finally investigated. As it turned out, I had the longest string of qualifications, among which was the bonus of possessing, as she described it, "a certain kind of face."

That bonus, actually, was the keystone of her whole project. One of the things that Lorraine had mastered during her acting years was the art of makeup. And I had the kind of face that easily lends itself to change. An artist would have told me that I was impossible to caricature because I had no outstanding features to build a caricature around. My features were all even, as she put it, well balanced and matched to one another. Not perfect features, she explained, like the old-time male ad models. Because perfect features lent themselves to caricature, too. Just nothing out of proportion. And it was helped by my coloring, my hair being neither blond nor brown but something nondescript and in-between. My skin, as she further noted, wasn't ruddy or dark, nor was it light and pale. Again, it was in-between. Now, why was all this important? It had to do with her skills at makeup, the basis of her grand scheme.

One morning, about two weeks after our first meeting, we were having breakfast together in her hotel room. No, I had not stayed overnight. We had not gotten that far yet. We had become friends and I had dropped by for morning coffee while, as she always did when we met, she continued with what she called my education.

"You know, like anything else, information has to be packed," she began on that occasion.

"Packed?" I repeated.

"Yes, *emballagé, non?*"

"I think you mean *packaged,*" I said.

"But of course." She gave a little nod, acknowledging the correction. "A good presentation is *de rigueur*. But the most important part of the presentation is not the technical part, the delivery system, the videos, the slides, the charts. That's the information. But who makes the presentation? Does this person have presence and authority, so they'll believe his slides and charts? This was what my special boardroom friend told me. Do you not know that many executives as well as politicians have coaches who teach them to be good performers, to have presence? For a time, I myself took such coaching jobs. My pupils included some of the most important people in the government of France, as well as executives of some of our largest corporations."

"But why?" I asked. "Surely you didn't need the money."

"I believed that the connections, as you call them, were important. For my plans. But, anyway, while I was doing it, I observed some of the results. I began more and more to realize that with real authority and presence—perhaps we should call it charisma?—such a person has only to whisper in the ear of his clients, and they've taken his information as gospel. His slides and charts are no longer part of the argument, but become matters of belief and guides to action. You see?"

I told her I didn't see. Because if she was referring to me, I couldn't meet the requirements.

"Again, think of your President Reagan. A very ignorant man. Half the time, asleep on the job. Not even a very good actor. And yet, consider how his most foolish words are received by so many with such enthusiasm. We can do even better than that. Do you see now?"

"Reagan does have presence, and the authority of office, if little else," I reminded her. "I don't."

"I can teach you to have presence as well as any executive or politician," she explained. "Very few are born with it. As for authority, all you need is the right air of mystery. If you are perceived as powerful and mysterious, you will have authority, believe me."

"But, my dear, I am not powerful and mysterious."

"A not-very-mysterious actor can perform the role of a powerful and mysterious personality very convincingly. Is it not so?"

"Lorraine, just exactly what are you getting at?"

"I will teach you to perform such a role. A change of name, a little manipulation of the press, coupled with some stories of impeccable sources of information . . ."

"How can I do that with Edward Horgan personally known to so many leading corporate clients? Is Edward Horgan supposed to disappear and then reappear disguised as some mysterious power broker from outer space?"

She laughed. "Outer space would be very impressive," she admitted. "But my skills do not reach so far. However, you won't have to live in disguise under your new identity. No, not with your special kind of face."

And then she laid it all out for me, her wild scheme with its weirdly ingenious method of making use of my "special kind of face."

Her plan was to *disguise Edward Horgan*. That way, in the new identity I was to assume later, I could live completely undisguised. I didn't understand at first. I confessed my confusion.

"It will take two years," she told me. "Every day for two years, I will change you just a little bit. In the meantime, you go about your regular business. No one will notice the changes. You know those hair products that men use to turn gray hair back to their original youthful colors, how they work so gradually no one ever notices, except they think you are looking better somehow? It is the same idea. After two years, you will not look like yourself. Then, when you become the mystery man we shall create, you can look like yourself again, no more makeup. Except you grow a beard. A natural beard.

It hides you a little and adds to the *mysterioso*. Yes? Maybe the worst that will happen, someone who knew you before the disguises started will say you look a little like someone they used to know. Also, I will work on your speech. You will, at the right time, have a proper way of sounding, not quite an accent."

"It sounds like a movie," I protested, even though I was charmed by the whole appalling idea.

She nodded eagerly. "Exactly—like a movie. Is that bad?"

I thought about it. "I doubt it'll work. And anyway, how would I get rid of Edward Horgan and become this mysterious new personality of authority and presence?"

"It is all carefully laid out in my plan."

Chapter Seven

Three months later, the plan went into operation, with a newspaper story reporting that Lorraine had married a certain wealthy Edouard Bazenrüd in a secret ceremony at Aix aux Bains. No one had ever heard of Bazenrüd, of course, because he was completely fictitious. However, the story was given credence at that time because Lorraine stood behind it, granting a very brief interview to the media at her home in the south of France. No pictures were permitted and Lorraine explained the absence of her husband with the statement that avoiding publicity was standard practice in the financial community of which he was a member.

Q: How can he avoid publicity if he's married to a film star?

A: I have made my last film. From now on, I shall work with my husband.

Q: Do you have the financial background for that?

A: Economics was my main interest before I became involved in cinema. I am merely going back to my original career choice.

Q: How long have you known Monsieur Bazenrüd?

A: We have been close for some time.

Q: Do you at least have some kind of photograph, something to show us what your husband looks like?

A: My husband would be very unhappy at having his picture appear in any public medium.

Since there were other financiers who also went to great pains to avoid publicity, this was not questioned too seriously. There wasn't much more to it than that. Lorraine simply refused to answer any questions beyond those needed to get the marriage mentioned in the press. She also explained that from now on, her life would be private and that this was her last interview.

The press obliged by printing the story that Lorraine had married "the mystery financier, Edouard Bazenrüd," and was retiring to private life. This was accompanied by a few speculative articles on the mystery man himself, carefully planted by Lorraine.

Her husband was the scion of a wealthy Hungarian family that had been virtually wiped out by the Nazis during World War II. Edouard, a mere six years old at the time, succeeded in escaping to England with an uncle who had contrived to convert a good portion of the family fortune into uncut diamonds. The subsequent death of that uncle left Edouard in comfortable circumstances, allowing him some years later to attend Harvard Business School under a pseudonym. This detail would provide an explanation for the occasional Americanisms that would be bound to slip through Bazenrüd's speech.

On his subsequent return to Europe, he went into financial banking. It was rumored that he had clients all over the Pacific rim and that his personal influence played a major role in banking circles throughout the developed world. In one of the articles, a well-known French politician, queried about Bazenrüd, said that while he was not personally acquainted with the man, he knew him by reputation and was prepared to vouch for Bazenrüd's impeccable standing in banking circles. That the politician had once been among those Lorraine had coached was never discovered by the press.

In the meantime, Lorraine had begun her slow transformation of my appearance. But I continued my normal business activities and, as Lorraine had predicted, no one really took any notice. At the end of six months, there was only a single incident involving an old acquaintance and business associate who had not seen me in all that time. He peered at me closely and remarked that something had happened to me.

"How do you mean?" I asked.

"I don't know. It's strange, but you look more—*spirituel.*"

"Ah, that. You're very perceptive, Claude. Yes, you might say I've had my midlife crisis. A real rite of passage. But it's all behind me now."

"What was our relationship?" As I tried to answer Kay's question, I clasped my hands together and shook them, an odd gesture I had picked up from Lorraine, which now bled through to my Alvin personality. I continued my story to Kay, but I still spoke in Edward's voice.

"We had become very close friends. It's possible we might have become lovers by then, but," again I made the gesture, "somehow, her bedroom–boardroom activities dulled my interest in that aspect. My middle-class puritanism was still quite active. Maybe we wouldn't even have become such close friends if our love affair hadn't been suspended for so long. Anyway, we set about developing the Bazenrüd reputation. As she'd planned it, I was to introduce her to a number of my leading clients when special opportunities arose."

One of the first of those clients, I went on, happened to be a major continental aluminum manufacturer who needed a large shipment of anhydrous bauxite to meet an emergency special order for the Soviet Union. The bauxite market was tight. Available supplies had been cornered by a U.S. competitor. Could I, Edward, solve the problem? Actually, I knew that there were large uncommitted supplies in Yugoslavia, but for political reasons, it seemed unlikely that they could be moved out of the country. The Yugoslav distribution system, never too good to begin with, was paralyzed by a struggle for control by rival Serb and Croat factions within the Party. But, I explained, there was a solution. There was one man who had the influence to get things moving within that difficult little nation. That man was Bazenrüd.

"Bazenrüd? Yes, I've heard of him. You know him? Would he be willing to help us?"

"I can arrange for Madame Bazenrüd to contact you. You can make all your arrangements through her."

It was an ideal situation for the success of Lorraine's plan. For in fact, the minister responsible for tying up the essential distribution system was an old bed companion. She knew she could influence him sufficiently to let through a large shipment of bauxite. And so she did, with the result that the needed bauxite was delivered and the name of Bazenrüd acquired new credence. But better than that, as soon as we knew the bauxite would become available, we made our moves in the commodities markets, short selling anhydrous bauxite since we knew the arrival of such a quantity on the market would certainly lower its price. By using a thousand Swiss francs to control a hundred thousand in the commodity, we were able to realize a hundredfold profit on our own activities.

Over the next two years, a number of similar incidents occurred where Bazenrüd was able to accomplish what no one else seemed able to manage. Not all of these successes could be attributed to Lorraine's sexual connections. There was one case in which an exorbitant bribe secured underwriting for a stock issue that no one wanted to touch.

This came about when an investigator employed by myself and Lorraine turned up the fact that a certain partner in an Amsterdam investment-banking house had dug himself into ruinous personal debt and had begun embezzling from his firm to remain solvent. The man, who would have appeared unbribable, proved all too malleable, since the bribe allowed him to rebalance his company's books. So the stock issue was underwritten, with results that were to prove disappointing later on for the stockholders. I had some doubts about letting this happen, but we did what we could to mitigate significant losses so that neither the client Bazenrüd served nor the bribed banker and his clients suffered any major consequences. Here too, there was the question of the larger mission that had to be weighed; and with some misgivings, we went ahead. I had learned long ago that moral decisions are never as clean-cut as we'd wish and in this case we acted as cleanly as pressing circumstances would permit. Lorraine and I, however, had contributed more to the bribe than we realized through the commission, a fact which disturbed me, but which Lorraine merely regarded as a further investment in building the Bazenrüd legend. "Besides," she reminded me, "our getting in on the initial public offering of the stock and then getting out before the crash completely shielded us from any real losses. Perhaps enough to recompense any clients who could not really absorb such costs."

By the end of two years, we had the rudiments of a permanent staff consisting of a statistician and a couple of first-rate programmers to work with the growing databases that were the foundation of our information management system. We had cultivated and trained a team of field investigators, and had put a certain Jean-Marc Robillard in charge of them.

Jean-Marc had been a stuntman during the filming of one of Lorraine's more successful features. He had come close to killing himself several times during the filming for which he received accolades from the producer and director. Only Lorraine noticed that the man took risks that went well beyond the requirements of his job. Her conclusion was that he was suicidal. She took him aside one afternoon during a lull in production and learned that he was suffering intensely over an unhappy love affair. From that day forward, she made it a point to spend time with him, to divert him with her own personal charm without ever becoming his lover. Her role, in fact, even though she was only two years his senior, was almost a motherly one.

It was not mere sentimentality that motivated her, but rather the fact that she recognized a certain broad talent in the man. He was Eurasian, the offspring of a marriage between circus people; he had a French father and a Chinese mother—from whom he'd actually acquired a working knowledge of Mandarin. On the other hand, he was almost completely European in appearance. He had a quick mind, a capacity for putting two and two together, a gift of observation that gave him astonishing insights into the character and behavior of most members of the film crew. Further, he combined toughness with a quality of loyalty that was rare. This was especially evident in the way he talked about the woman who had betrayed him.

Lorraine, in the end, encouraged him to abandon his work as a stuntman and provided him with the backing to set up his own investigative service, introducing him to the right people so that he was soon able to win contracts with corporations plagued by industrial espionage. Eight months into his new career, when Lorraine formed her strange alliance with me, she sent for Jean-Marc and made him chief of the investigative team she was forming. When she discovered that he liked me, she allowed him, without a second thought, into the secrets of our association. He became the general factotum, chauffeur, chief investigator, bodyguard and, to some extent, even occasional advisor to us both, particularly on matters Asian, where his knowledge of Mandarin proved highly valuable.

All operations at this time were conducted from the Bazenrüd Geneva office run by Lorraine in the role of Madame Bazenrüd. Only Jean-Marc knew why Edouard Bazenrüd never put in an appearance there.

Chapter Eight

I could tell that Kay, instead of getting sleepy during this long narration, was becoming more alert. Normally, she retires early, being an early riser. I'm much the opposite. But her attention had been so caught by the intimations of Edward's personality breaking through into my Alvin personality, that I knew she had become extremely uncomfortable as I continued talking about Lorraine. I offered to postpone it. She wouldn't have it. She wanted to hear it all, now.

I tried to remind her of what Thongden had shown me: that none of our personalities were real, but insofar as they were forms we created to conduct specific lives, it was important not to attribute feelings from a different life as pertinent to our current lives. I tried to persuade her that my Alvin self had nothing to do with Lorraine. That Lorraine belonged entirely to Edward's life. Her discomfort therefore was about as irrelevant to us as news stories of the infidelities and sexual involvements of members of the British royal family. "Somehow, I'm not so sure," Kay said, glaring at me with a mixture of perplexity and asperity. "This whole transformation scene she proposed for you—it just doesn't seem plausible."

"I guess it doesn't. I don't know what I can do to convince you," I admitted.

"Maybe if you could go more into detail."

I shrugged. Perhaps, from her point of view, it was a reasonable request. I settled back on the rocking chair facing the place on the couch to which she now seemed to cling as to a small island of reality in a sea of confusion.

I proceeded to explain to her how some of the makeup Lorraine used on me, that is, on Edward Horgan, was semipermanent. She didn't have to renew it more than once a month. But a lot of it did have to be touched up each morning. So I would sit in front of that three-sided makeup mirror in our little "safe house," to borrow an epithet from the espionage vernacular, a place known only to ourselves and Jean-Marc, and watch her repairing the old and adding subtle new changes to my face.

All the time, during every moment of it, I continued to find it hard to believe that I was really doing this. Those little tricks of color she used on my skin and my hair, the eyebrow treatments, the tonsorial restyling that changed the shape of my face, my mouth. She even knew how to alter the appearance of my teeth. My upper incisors had a normal slight separation at the center, which she eliminated by the use of a semipermanent dental plastic. She was remarkably skilled. She also worked on my French; at this I was quite fluent, but she was trying to get me to learn how to speak it with a slight Hungarian accent. Naturally not for present use, but for the day when Bazenrüd would appear on the scene. But I kept asking myself, why am I doing this? Why am I so readily participating in this gradual erasure of Edward Horgan? Do I really believe in this tenuous notion that we are building up our forces to resist a coming assault that I can neither describe nor express in any way that makes sense?

One morning, I instructed my cabby to drive on ahead a few blocks and pick me up later along the way. I wanted to walk. There was a freshness in the air that seemed to rise up from the lake with a kind of crystalline purity that stretched across the whole city so that the sun just above the eastern horizon looked like a newly minted gold piece. A light breeze came from the north, bringing odors of damp pine and awakening ancient nostalgias of cool afternoons in the Vermont countryside when my young son, Jack, would trudge along at my side and I would point things out to him: the return of a kingbird who had built a nest on the crossbars of the telephone pole outside our house; the first trillia shyly blossoming amid the ferns around the white maple, on whose branches the red buds were already bursting into leaves.

Erase Edward Horgan, I thought, and all of this remains untouched. And anyway, Edward Horgan would have gone on changing naturally. This was only a speeding up of the process, a humanly contrived technique of reincarnation which, in the end, would transform me into someone called Bazenrüd.

And yet, everything else remains the same, the memories, the dreams, the hopes. So what does it matter if they happen to belong to Bazenrüd rather than Edward Horgan? There is that fundamental *I* who is clearly neither. And yet again, in some vague superstitious way, I was nervous about it all, as though I were indulging in some daring *hubris* for which I would pay dearly in the end. Besides, the long process of transformation tested my patience. There were moments when I felt I was participating in a very childish game and wondered how I'd ever let her talk me into it.

What really was her influence over me? We weren't even lovers. I think we had both decided that some distance was needed between us for the sake of the partnership. Besides, I found it difficult to reconcile myself to her past. I also felt that if I let myself go, I might find myself absolutely enmeshed with her. She had an almost vulpine attraction which I constantly worked hard to minimize.

At the same time, I could not really open myself to any other relationships, because my makeup could not be concealed during such intimacies. My only recourse was to the occasional bordello where my anonymity and my eccentricities were respected, a very unsatisfactory compromise for a man like myself. As a result, I had gone from enjoying a reasonably active sex life to having a mostly celibate existence. The effects were strange. There was an odd sense of freedom. It was apparently quite true that a voluntary abstinence reallocates the energies; sublimation, to use the not-so-fashionable Freudian term, was producing in my case a kind of low-level euphoria. I mean, it was always lurking beneath the surface—a sense of possibility, even an intimation of joy. My concentration was better. The world looked more roseate.

But there were long periods during my waking day when the underlying euphoria was not at the center of my attention. I would sit in the office of a client, feeling a little ridiculous beneath the latest additions to my makeup, and wondering, whenever he looked at me, whether he was going to make some remark about my altered appearance. Of course, it never happened. Lorraine had done her work too well for that. But it was at times like these that I would again begin questioning my reasons for doing all this.

It had been going on now for over a year. And I didn't really feel quite like myself anymore. Even though reason dictated that I remained the same whether my name was Horgan or Bazenrüd, there seemed to be more to it than that. I found there was far more to the particular than I'd ever imagined. As though, without my own established specificity, I seemed to live, move, and work behind some sort of cloudy screen from which I could look out but no one could really look in. It was very much like being intoxicated, but it wasn't always pleasant. The longer it went on, the more uncomfortable it got. So even though it was all working out as planned, with Bazenrüd's reputation and reality growing ever larger among important corporate movers and shakers, I again began to ask myself what I ultimately hoped to get out of it.

But the question was wrong. I knew that. There was nothing for me to get out of it. It was part of something I had to do, a duty that was laid on me. Without quite being able to explain it more fully, I was convinced that it had something to do with who I was, part of the baggage of being Edward Horgan. More puzzling, though, was why I had only recently begun to feel that way. Was it something Lorraine had awakened in me, or even, had transmitted to me with that intimation of dark forces that needed to be held back? I was a practical man, or at least I always had been until Lorraine had come into my life. And I needed to know more about whatever we were pitted against. I needed specifics, particularities, names, persons.

One afternoon, I demanded a clearer answer from her. We were just sitting down in my office to discuss certain business matters, but I brushed those aside and came right out with what was troubling me. Her response surprised me.

"I have been waiting for you to ask such a question," she said, settling herself rather primly across from me at the round conference table, her hands crossed. "I would have been disappointed had you not asked."

"May I allow myself to be flabbergasted once again?" I said.

"But truly, since I have built such great expectations upon you, I would not have wanted you to be the kind of man who would go blindly along with our performance because it is amusing, not to mention financially rewarding. I had always seen you as one much above such trivial concerns."

"Whether that's the case or not," I said, "I feel that our original grand purpose has somehow been pushed aside. Or perhaps, to put it more precisely, faded from view."

"And what about *your* purpose?" she challenged me. "I had understood that you also sensed an importance in our efforts. Has not that importance sharpened for you? Has it not become clearer?"

"If it had, I wouldn't be questioning you now."

"You no longer feel the imminence of those dangers you once seemed to recognize?"

"I've thought about it. And I'm willing to concede that the world is a dangerous place. But it's always been dangerous. Skipping all the small stuff and just looking at the Thirty Years War, the two World Wars, and now, the Cold War with the doomsday clock still ticking, are we going to change anything after all this time?"

"The Thirty Years War was a bad time," she acknowledged. "Interesting that you should have mentioned just that time, because we are coming to something like it again."

"I don't think so," I said. "In fact, the reverse is probably true. If you're right and the Cold War really ends, very likely we will see a period of greater peace and internationalism than ever before. If you're right," I repeated pointedly.

"We will see the breaking out of every cause, every ethnic hatred, every fundamentalism that has been restrained by the Cold War. We will see chaos, terrorism, and a complete abandonment of civility. On all continents, except perhaps Australia. I tell you that now, knowing I cannot convince you. It is too soon. But we cannot stop that. It is too much for us. During this time, the great corporations will lose all restraint and drive their workers back to the slavery of the early industrial revolution. That, too, we cannot stop. But there is something else, perhaps worse. And now I can tell you from where it will come."

"Lorraine, these are wild statements. How can you sound so sure?"

She ignored my question and began on an entirely different tack. "In China, by the end of this century, there will be a billion and a half people. The southern part will be rich and prosperous, but the rest of China will lack food and water. Water, let me tell you, will be far more precious than oil. The present regime will try brutally to maintain order. But it will have only secular means at its disposal. And it will fail until it draws from the wisdom of China's past the support of forces of a different order." At this, she broke off and looked at me.

I shook my head. "You can't know all this. No one can."

She continued to sit there with her hands clasped, looking at me. "It is not exactly a thing like knowledge," she explained. "Not exactly that at all. It has more to do with the way events are constructed."

I was pulled from the midst of my narration by a sudden interruption from Kay. "Wait," she said. "Wait."

I came back to myself across a long divide. I had been so caught up with speaking in Edward's voice that I needed a moment to get back to myself. "Yes?" I asked, finally. "What?"

"What you just told me. What Lorraine said. How could she have said that?"

"Said what?"

"She said, 'It's not exactly a thing like knowledge.' And then she said something about it having to do with the way events are constructed. That's exactly what Thongden said. Word for word. At least, that's what you told me."

Even as she was saying it, I knew she was right. And I remembered the rest of what Thongden had said: *In the multilayered universe, as it really exists, there are clumps of events that belong together, that are related in a kind of noncausal grouping, their connection having to do with value and meaning rather than material events.* A multiple bleedthrough had taken place, and it involved my Alvin self along with Edward and Lorraine. It was not in any way connected with reincarnation. Not in a universe which, as Thongden had explained, everything is happening at once. What connected particular lives, regardless of their apparent positioning on the timescale, was a community of meaning, of shared values and purposes.

And I also understood at that moment that because Edward was in some way part of me, I was also part of him, and that was how, at his own proper moment, he had to have become aware of me. But, in Edward's experience, that was still some way off. I looked at Kay, feeling tempted to get ahead of my story and tell her how it happened. But I thought better of it. Better to take it step by step if I didn't want her to become utterly confused.

"He wasn't aware of me as Alvin just at that point," I explained to Kay. "And neither was Lorraine. So she didn't know she was quoting Thongden, or that there'd been a bleedthrough from me. Later, Edward would realize it. But Lorraine never needed to become conscious of me. Being a *sensitif,* she was used to knowing things without knowing their source."

Kay continued to sit there, watching me with a mixture of wonder and bewilderment, still trying to get it all straight in her mind.

"And at that moment, it's also true that I, or Edward rather, was aware of Alvin only indirectly, as a kind of nervous resistance to his business certainties, a background element he had to keep from becoming obtrusive. And also to some extent Edward was aware of Alvin as sharing with him another force connected with that resistance. That force, for me, was my Batman phantasm. A kind of strength that I couldn't use because I had rejected it. But Edward was aware of it—it's difficult to explain this—as a strength. A capacity for acting with great power, since he didn't suffer from the financial inhibitions that I had all mixed up with Batman, that for me made Batman, or rather, my image of Batman, such a negative figure. But I can see this is terribly confusing for you. Let me get on with the story. As it unfolds, you'll begin to understand. Okay?"

"No, not okay," my wife replied. "I need to know how Lorraine knew. How was she able to repeat Thongden's words?"

"Ah, that." I shook my head. "I thought I explained it, that as a *sensitif,* Lorraine could sort of pick things out of the air. She was closer to Edward than either of them realized. Kind of destined for him, you might say. So she was psychically sensitive to what he knew."

"But Edward didn't know Thongden either."

"Oh yes he did. But it happened in a strange way. Much later on. It wouldn't make any sense if I revealed it to you now before I told you what led up to it. Remember, Edward Horgan or Bazenrüd is very different from me. What we shared was a kind of common financial interest, except that mine is kind of all tied up in personal psychological problems. In fact, Edward was supposed to be the one to help me solve them, according to Thongden. But as Edward, I was still in the stage where I was trying to get a handle on my relationship with Lorraine." I had fallen back into my Edward voice even as I tried to explain things. And Kay let me go on without any further interruption.

As Edward, I explained to Kay, I felt a heightened kind of awareness when I was with Lorraine. There were times when we were walking together that I'd have the impulse to hold her hand. I never did, actually, although I didn't feel she'd object. I knew what it was. I remembered, in my innocence, feeling that way in the later grades of primary school about a succession of girls. Puppy love. I was going through a late phase of puppy love and was content to let it remain innocent that way. After all, it was a wonderful thing for a fully grown man to experience. But of course, when she wasn't around, I felt more and more that I wouldn't be able to put up with the whole charade for another day. From hour to hour my feelings contradicted themselves, swinging wildly back and forth. It was too much.

In the end I put up with it for almost two years. In the meantime, Britain had gotten herself into the Falklands War. This only became a matter of concern to me when I received a call at my Geneva office from an assistant undersecretary at the British Foreign Office, a man named Hightrestle.

Was it not true that I had once secured a certain rare steel alloy for a certain French industrial company? Before admitting that I had, which was surely known to my caller or he wouldn't have been phoning me, I remembered that the company in question was the builder and manufacturer of France's deadly Exocet missile. I had heard on the morning news that such a missile in Argentine hands had yesterday sunk a British frigate.

"Yes," I admitted. "I'm the one."

"Mr. Horgan, would you come to Whitehall for an important meeting?"

"Concerning the same French company?"

"We would prefer to discuss it in person. Will you come, Mr. Horgan?"

"I can't give you any information on the Exocet worth the trip."

"We know that. Will you come?"

"Tell me when and I'll check my schedule and—"

He interrupted swiftly. "We should like you to come at once."

"At once?"

"Both Her Majesty and Mrs. Thatcher wish it known that you will find it most rewarding."

Although very fluent in the language of the corporate executive suite, I was less well equipped to interpret the niceties of diplomatic language. Nevertheless, I understood that Hightrestle, by specifically mentioning the prime minister and the queen, was saying more than I fully grasped. I agreed to take the next flight out and present myself at Whitehall that same afternoon. But first I telephoned Lorraine at her own office nearby, the new premises of Bazenrüd SA.

"Make your flight arrangements, but stop by here on your way to the airport."

A half-hour later, I was dismissing my cab at Lorraine's address. Jean-Marc Robillard was watching at the curb for me. He took my arm and led me to her sedan, parked a few yards back. She was waiting for me in the rear seat. I climbed in beside her while Jean-Marc got behind the wheel.

"We can talk on the way to the airport. You understand what is being offered?" Lorraine said

I shook my head. "I'm not sure."

"No, you probably wouldn't," she said, smiling at me. Then, changing the subject, "You will be interested to know that our British friends are not having much success in persuading the French to stop further shipments of Exocet missiles to Argentina."

"How do you know all this?"

"I have just been on the phone to one of my friends in Paris." She used the French expression, *un ami,* which was more explicit than *un de mes amis.* "Actually, the French feel that this is Mrs. Thatcher's war, being waged to bolster her declining popularity, and they are rather disinclined to comply with British requests. The French case is made easier by the fact that the missiles, ordered before the Falklands trouble, are now on a ship bound for Argentina. And the British are not really prepared to stop and board a French vessel on the high seas. A true diplomatic impasse, you see?"

"But what can I possibly do about it?"

Lorraine shrugged. "You have good relations with the manufacturer of the Exocet?"

I nodded. "What if I do? They can't recall an order authorized by the French government."

"No, but think. Is there not something you can perhaps provide them? These munitions makers are always suffering shortages of critical materials. Copper perhaps? Or manganese?"

"No shortage of either of those today. I suppose I could perhaps find something to bribe them with, you're right, there's always something or other they'd like to stockpile. But how could that give them any leverage with the French government? No, as far as I'm concerned, it's a useless trip."

"You give up too quickly. Is there not some weapon, some armament the French government is ready to produce, but lacks materials for?"

"You mean, can I provide some component that is holding up production of a planned weapons system? Like what? You're getting far too complicated. Even with a system that's ready for production, do you know how long it takes just to set up Quality Assurance norms?"

"Perhaps not." She paused in thought for a moment; then she put a hand on my arm. "They offered you a knighthood. Did you understand that?"

"Is that what it was?" I laughed. "What would I want with a bloody knighthood?"

"It would suit Bazenrüd very well."

"I hardly think he could get himself knighted in absentia."

"No, not in absentia." Again that pressure of her hand on my arm.

"Me? Wait a minute. You're jumping way ahead of yourself. You want me to tell them that Bazenrüd will handle it? Then you show up, representing him, and he solves everything? And I show up as Bazenrüd and accept the knighthood? Great. Can you tell me how? Have you got the least idea what you're promising to do?"

"A least idea, yes. Possibly."

In the dimness of the rear of that car, I could see her watching me speculatively.

"You mentioned Quality Assurance," she said. "This is the process that guarantees that all steps in the production follow definite, clear procedures. Yes?"

"Yes. You've done your homework."

"And there are little slips, signed by every person involved in the process, to assure that all steps have been observed properly?"

"Yes," I acknowledged. "Where do you get all this information?"

"From books. And at this manufacturer of the Exocet, there is someone in charge of these slips?"

"The Quality Assurance manager for the company."

"He is the same one who handles Quality Assurance for the missile?"

"Not necessarily. But he could be. What are you getting at, Lorraine?"

"But he might know the person who handles Quality Assurance for the missile?"

"Very likely. Quality Assurance people like to exchange ideas with one another. In fact, they're kind of clubby, since they're constantly getting pressured by the rest of management, who don't always understand what they do."

"You know this man?"

"I helped the QA manager set up some of the necessary procedures for working with the special steel alloy I procured for them. Yes, I know that one well enough. But what about it?"

She evaded my question. She was already looking out the window as Jean-Marc turned onto the airport entrance road. "You must tell Whitehall that you can't handle it yourself, and then suggest Bazenrüd. Just as you've done before."

"Now wait. Unless you really have a solution up that fine silken sleeve of yours, it's too much of a risk."

"I think there is a solution. We will discuss it further when you return."

"I need to know now."

"There's no time."

"Lorraine, I—"

"Do it. I promise it will work out."

The car had stopped and Jean-Marc was already opening the door for me. I grabbed my attaché case and, without another word, headed into the airport departure lounge.

* * *

Robert Hightrestle was a short, stout man in his late fifties with the iciest blue eyes I had ever seen. His small pupils added a certain fine penetration to his gaze, so that when he looked at me, I felt as though I were being probed by a pair of lasers even as he leaned across his desk and gripped my palm in a hand like glass. For a moment, I was absolutely convinced that now, at last, someone was seeing through my disguise. In the rush of the day, we had slipped up. Lorraine hadn't done her usual retouching job this morning, she was so anxious to get me off to my plane.

"Good of you to look in," Hightrestle said, releasing my hand and motioning me to a chair. He sat down himself and thrust his thumbs behind his braces as he leaned back in his chair. "There's tea on the way. Meantime, let's get down to cases. No time for amenities on this one. We're really under pressure. Understood, old boy?" Without giving me time to reply, he lifted a sheet from his desk and while seeming to scan it, said, "You've got very close ties, a good friendship really, with Monsieur Armand Jolicoeur, chief of metallurgy at Techno-Mondiale in Paris. Jolicoeur also happens to be the son-in-law of the chairman of the board of the parent company, right?"

"Which produces the Exocet missile. Right," I said with a faint sardonic undertone. "But I haven't been in touch with Armand lately." I had a feeling as I said this that he would know I was lying. That sheet of paper he was scanning probably covered the facts quite accurately. But I was setting the stage for Bazenrüd as Lorraine had requested, so I decided to brazen it through by establishing that I was not the man he wanted.

"Our information is that you've been in contact as recently as a week ago."

"Your information is incorrect then," I announced. I had already learned from Lorraine and corroborated from my own experience that information in the corporate world is no stronger than one's ability to affirm it. Deny it forcefully enough and the information easily comes into question. "I haven't seen Armand in a year. But how does my relationship with him concern you?"

"It's a matter of what your former President Eisenhower called the 'military industrial complex'," he began. "In short, in the area of weapons manufacture, the boardroom, the generals, and the chamber of deputies are all part of the same tight-knit little club. Armand Jolicoeur's father-in-law began his career as an upper-grade civil servant in the War Department. Even though he was not a socialist, his friendship with François Mitterand was well known. Before Mitterand became president, of course. So it occurred to us that any possible influence you could exert personally on Jolicoeur would eventually reach Mitterand. Indeed, we were wondering whether you might not in fact be willing to offer Jolicoeur, in return for his cooperation, access to a very substantial stockpile of—" And here, he thrust a sheet of paper at me on which was written only a single word, the chemical name of an element vital to the manufacture of certain sophisticated detonating devices in both a conventional and nuclear environment. I whistled.

"We have a corner on the market, you know," Hightrestle said.

I admitted I hadn't been aware of it.

"It's an excellent quid pro quo, wouldn't you say?"

I nodded. "With this," I said, thrusting the paper back at him, "why can't you make a deal with Mitterand directly?"

"Impossible. Mitterand has closed any diplomatic channel for discussion on the Exocet. He has his own political reasons. The nudge would have to come from his close contacts with the manufacturer. In fact, it's a bit of a long shot, but given your reputation, your reputation for acting swiftly—as you must realize, time is of the essence—we thought that you might be the man to set things in motion."

I stared down at the desk in an effort to project by my long silence that I was carefully considering the matter. Finally I said, "I don't think I can help you with Armand. But . . ."

Hightrestle turned his laser stare onto high intensity. "But what?"

"You've heard of Edouard Bazenrüd, of course?" As I said it, I found myself hoping that Lorraine knew what the hell she was doing. Because otherwise, I was walking over a cliff.

"Bazenrüd? Well, yes, we've heard of him," Hightrestle admitted. "But we really don't know a thing about him. Anyway, I don't see how he could get any kind of handle on this particular situation."

"You sent for me, to solicit my help. Bazenrüd is my best recommendation," I insisted.

Again Hightrestle consulted his long sheet of paper. "Do you know Bazenrüd personally?"

"I've never met him. Very few do. But I do know Madame Bazenrüd, who usually acts as his agent. I see her occasionally in the normal course of business. Actually, our Geneva offices are reasonably nearby."

"Do you mean that if Bazenrüd gets involved, you'll be working with him? We would consider that, since we know you. But otherwise . . ."

"Bazenrüd, as you may have heard, has methods of working that require his operating entirely alone. Both for his protection and that of his clients."

His discomfiting gaze seemed to divert itself from me for an instant. Then he nodded and rubbed his fingers upward along the side of his shiny, well-shaven cheek as though checking for any errant beard growth. "In that case, I'm afraid we'll have to look elsewhere," he said.

"If you should change your mind," I said, "you can contact him through Madame Bazenrüd at their Geneva office. Otherwise he'd be impossible to find. Just in case, there's a special private number I can give you."

"Why not?" Hightrestle said, offering me his glassy hand again.

"We do appreciate your looking in, Horgan. Sure you won't stay for tea?"

I was back in Geneva late that same afternoon. But events had already preceded me. Hightrestle had called Lorraine on the special line almost immediately after I'd left his office. But even before the call came, Lorraine had been busy. She called me at home from her office the minute I stepped inside. "We must meet immediately," she informed me. I was taken aback by her unexpectedly brusque tone.

"Is something wrong?" I asked.

"At L'Abris," she said, referring to our safe house and evading my question for the time being.

I hurried over and found her waiting for me. "Why did you not tell me about your good friend Armand Jolicoeur?"

It was hard to know whether she was angry, or merely disapproving, or simply curious. She stood there and looked at me with an expression I found impossible to read.

"It never came up."

"Don't be evasive with me, Edward. When we discussed Quality Assurance at the missile company, it would have been appropriate for you to mention that you had even higher connections there. Why did you not?"

I moved past her and settled down on the sofa at the end of the room. "Okay," I admitted. "I didn't mention Armand because I was afraid you might try to bribe him. Or get at him some other way."

"And if I had?" Her tone was so far no more than curious. There was nothing of anger or even disapproval. Only a certain implacability. I realized I would have to explain fully.

"Armand is completely unreachable," I told her. "He is a man of unimpeachable integrity. It would have been a waste of time to bring his name up during our hurried trip to the airport."

"There was certainly time to tell me all this. I wouldn't have had to waste time to find it out for myself."

"You had him checked out? But how did you know I—?"

"You forget that I already know so much about you. Your friendship with Armand turned up in the computer when I went to check on your Quality Assurance manager."

As she said this, it suddenly struck me that she had not been altogether open with me—not while she maintained a dossier on me that I hadn't even known about until now. That was when it also became clear to me that she had been using my rather jejune attachment to her as a means of dominating our relationship, both business and personal. For the first time since I had known her, I was suddenly very angry.

"You didn't try to approach Armand on your own, did you?" I demanded.

"No, but I made inquiries. You are very disapproving, Edward."

"Yes," I said bluntly. "I disapprove of your keeping a private file on me without my knowledge or consent. I disapprove of your investigating a personal friend. And now that I consider it, I disapprove of your constantly making decisions without consulting me first."

"Aah. Should I have phoned you at Whitehall before I looked into Armand?"

"And if you'd found him reachable, would you have acted before consulting me?"

"This is academic. Besides, we do not have all the time in the world."

At that moment, as I looked at her, I seemed to undergo a change of vision. I remembered, some ten years earlier, when I had accompanied a lady friend to an optometrist's shop, how, while she was being tested, the optometrist came up alongside me as I sat reading a magazine in his waiting room and thrust a lens between my eyes and the printed page. I don't know what insight into my visual capacities the man possessed—perhaps it was the distance at which I held the page from my eyes, or perhaps he did this to everyone who visited his shop—but I was suddenly and unexpectedly made aware of how hazy the print had become for me by the sudden clarity with which that strip of glass displayed it. On that occasion, I had ordered my first set of reading glasses on the spot. And somehow, when Lorraine presented me with the facts of her investigation of Armand and her computer dossier on me, it was again as if a lens had been passed before my eyes. And there she was, clearly revealed to me for the first time. My passivity toward her managing of my affairs, even my childish fixation on her, vanished like figments of a dream I had for too long carried over into my real life. I felt both aroused and challenged.

"If you had taken the trouble to consult me," I declared, "we might have saved precious time. There are much better ways than going after the chief contractor for the missile."

She stood watching me, her hands raised in a gesture of self-deprecation (was I to take it as a sort of apology?) as she said, "I'm consulting you now."

"There are many subcontractors, the small companies who worked on essential parts of the missile—the guidance system, for example. Certain motherboards in that system are produced by small computer companies where security is much more lax, and it's possible to reach almost anyone you need to reach." I didn't realize it then, but I was thinking as she had taught me to think, with no scruples to muddy my planning.

"But they have no influence. They are too far removed from the government."

I took her by the hand and drew her down alongside me on the small couch that faced the window looking out toward the lake. The sky was already darkening on the opposite shore. "You were talking about Quality Assurance before. Let's talk about it some more. There has to be a QA record even with the small contractors. Like the company that makes the motherboard for the guidance system. It's part of the process."

"You're suggesting some kind of manipulation of the QA system?"

I had the glimmerings of an idea, but it hadn't taken shape yet. "Of course," I said, "let's say we could get someone in such a company to alter the QA slips. If the missile were still in production, we'd be able to use that to halt production. But so far, I can't see how it'll bring back the missiles already aboard ship."

"You can't?" she exclaimed. "Of course you can. Even I can. If you're able to stop production, you can also stop delivery. France can't afford to deliver a flawed product that wouldn't function properly."

"And if one slip were altered," I added with growing excitement, unaware of how hard I was squeezing her hand, "and someone were to stumble on the alteration and report it as a possible production error . . ."

". . . They'd have to recall the shipment before it got delivered."

"What if we can't get things moving before the shipment is delivered?"

"Even then, the Argentines would have to be warned by the French government. So they wouldn't dare use the missiles. But our real problem is locating the right subcontractor and then getting to work on whoever handles the QA data file."

"That's the least of our problems," I said. "The whole idea came to me because I already know about the motherboard and who makes it. Armand happened to mention it months ago, when I secured that alloy for his company."

Suddenly sitting there side by side on the couch, we found ourselves staring into one another's eyes in wonder. That was when I took her face in my hands and kissed her for the first time. It was a heady moment, but brief: the sealing of a new compact. When I drew back, I said, "But first off, I want to look at everything you keep in those files of yours, especially on me."

After that, we proceeded with the details of dealing with whomever we would get within the company to alter the QA slips. We decided that a bribe of some magnitude would be the simplest and shortest route. But we had to be sure of our man. There was then the question of whether that same man should be used to report finding the "error," or whether we could rely on a standard periodic process review to turn up the error in the normal course of events. Such a process review is a Quality Assurance must. It's a kind of final screening, an effort to catch errors even after the fact. It would have been the best way for us, but it depended on when the next process review was scheduled. Too long a wait would rule that avenue out. But our first step was a closer investigation of the company. We called in Jean-Marc and told him to get the investigative team on it at once.

It took almost two days for the wheels to turn. But in the meantime, another factor intervened, one that I hadn't anticipated, and for which I felt extremely ill prepared.

I had joined Lorraine at L'Abris for my early morning touch-up. As yet, we had had no report from our investigators. I sat down before the table with its trifold mirror and waited for her to begin.

"This time," she told me, "it's going to be very different."

"How much is 'very'? A bigger nose?" I joked. "You have some plan to make my ears stick out, make me ugly so no other woman will look at me?"

"No, today we're going to improve you. Today, we're changing you back to yourself."

I didn't understand. "Myself?"

"The way you looked two years ago, when I first met you."

"You mean . . ." I hesitated. "Now?"

She put her head down close to mine as we stared at our two faces in the mirror. "Do you remember what you looked like?"

"I'm not sure. But, what does all this mean?"

This time it was she who took my face in her hands. "The way I like you best," she said, "is as yourself."

"But—"

"Don't you understand? You don't need the disguise anymore. It's time for Edouard Bazenrüd to appear onstage."

In spite of the warm feeling of her hands on my cheeks, I felt a chill of fear. "Are you telling me that you are not the one who's going to show up at Whitehall?"

"I do not think your friend Hightrestle will appreciate Madame Bazenrüd putting in an appearance instead of her husband."

"Why not? I prepared the ground well. I convinced him that Bazenrüd rarely presents himself in person. I—"

"You are forgetting, *mon cher,* there's a knighthood in this for you. And that knighthood will increase Bazenrüd's credibility a thousandfold. But he has to show himself to accept it."

"But that's a way off. Months, before I even get on the royal calendar. Besides, this Hightrestle practically has X-ray eyes. He'll recognize me in a minute. Believe me. You should've seen him."

Suddenly she laughed. "I will make a bet with you. If you recognize yourself, I won't insist that you go. Now, turn around this way. Let's get started. But first, put these on." And she handed me a pair of blinders. "I do not want you to see the changes until all is finished. Then you can decide."

Chapter Nine

"Something wrong?" I said to Kay. "You've been giving me funny looks for the last ten minutes."

She waved her hands in some confusion. "I'm not really sure anymore who I'm listening to. Is it you, or Edward Horgan? When you started telling about how . . ." She hesitated, and blinked her eyes at me a couple of times before going on: ". . . how you kissed her for the first time."

Suddenly I laughed. I'm afraid it was an artificial-sounding laugh. There was no relaxation in her gaze.

"You keep confusing me with Horgan. But we're not the same person. I'll admit I get carried away when I describe the details of that other life. Maybe, for moments while I'm talking, I almost sound like Horgan. But it worked the same way, when I was Horgan."

"You mean, you remembered who you really were?"

"Who I really am isn't Alvin *or* Horgan. You have to remember that. But I'd have a sense of my Alvin personality, often very strongly, during all that time as Horgan. Mostly in strange dreams, where I'd remember a self that was living here, in this house. With you. It was a very powerful bleedthrough. So in a way, I had some profound if dormant sense that I was living another life, or at least more than one life at the same time. Also, during those moments of recollection, I'd experience a strong yearning for my Alvin life. Even a sense of loss. Of missing something important."

"You really did?"

"It's not surprising, is it, considering?"

She seemed pacified, at least for the moment. She asked me to get back to Horgan's story.

I agreed, but not before asking her to promise not to get me confused with Horgan, who was now about to become Bazenrüd. Once again, I began to describe how Lorraine set about accomplishing that minor miracle. I again assumed Edward's point of view.

It took Lorraine the better part of six hours. She began with the unpleasant process of undying my hair, which she had darkened incrementally from month to month. Then she restyled it, cutting it back to the shorter length at which I had originally worn it. She worked on my mouth, my teeth; she removed a pair of thin false lashes from my eyelids. She had long ago begun applying a brown dye for mottling the back of my hands and giving them a more hirsute appearance by darkening their small blonde tufts of hair. Now she swabbed it all away with a grayish liquid that smelled of acetone. She even cut my nails, which I had allowed to grow longer. She had also placed a ruby ring in a large tasteless gold setting on my pinky, to contrast with the fact that I never wore jewelry of any kind. This was followed by a lot of additional swabbing of my face where she had overlaid a certain tanning substance with minute shadings of pink and blue along the cheeks and jawline to alter the contour of my face.

She had long since done away with my reading glasses, substituting over my protests contact lenses which I found a nuisance to take care of. These she had changed every few months with lenses of an ever-deepening shade, slowly altering the color of my eyes from their natural gray to brown. She now had me remove the blinders just long enough for me to extract the contact lenses, requiring me to turn my head away from the mirror lest I see myself before the transformation was complete.

As I sat through the long procedure, I began to realize how many incremental changes she had made during the past two years, accomplishing them so gradually that I myself hardly noticed the difference, except for the mounting inconveniences they caused me—which was exactly why the whole thing had worked so well. Because no one else had really noticed the difference either.

But now that the process was being reversed, I again found myself wondering why I had ever submitted to it and what led me to believe the gain would be worth all the trouble. The question that sprang to mind now was, How much difference would there actually turn out to be? Would I see in the original Edward Horgan, to whom she was restoring me, the same Edward Horgan I was now? How much alteration would time itself have made in the original model?

I had some old photographs with which I compared myself from time to time, but they went back more than a decade. I normally submitted to being photographed only at very long intervals, and it would have been difficult to recognize me as quite the same person in any case. Nevertheless, since I knew what I looked like then, I could still make out the lineaments of the real me somewhat dimly beneath a lot of the façade Lorraine had imposed. At the same time, in trying to be objective about it, I had had to admit that over time it had become more and more difficult to recognize myself. But since I would soon be facing a crucial test by exposure to Hightrestle's acute glances, I now grew impatient to see myself stripped and pared down to the original Edward Horgan.

But even though she had finished working on my head and hands, Lorraine insisted that I remain blindered while she helped me into a change of clothes. Even in this, she had been meticulous, having gradually imposed changes of style on the way I normally dressed with which I never felt truly comfortable. She had made me wear vested suits with longer jackets than had been to my taste, and cut and shaped in a manner that made me appear significantly heavier. She arranged to have my trousers gradually break at a lower point over my shoe, explaining that the way a man's pants hung was so distinctively personal that it became an important element of recognition. She even introduced a slight sag around my seat to which my vanity had never become reconciled, even though the day-to-day changes were almost imperceptible. She had put me into starched white shirts with long cuffs bearing ornamental links, instead of my own favored striped and colored oxfords with their soft button-down collars and button cuffs.

My shoe styles too were gradually altered. I had always favored a kind of low-cut, crepe-soled shoe, usually in a tan or brown. Even at formal occasions, when I was forced to wear black, my shoes were made of kid leathers built over a soft rubber sole. Actually, I had always had tender feet, and the heavier, more conventional black brogans that Lorraine had required me to adopt were responsible for a variety of calluses and a few tender toe joints. Eventually she found a bootmaker who knew how to modify the inside of a shoe to protect a sensitive wearer and, at the same time, add additional height, which was augmented with each new pair until an inch-and-a-half accretion had been achieved.

Altogether, she had turned me into a rather stodgy, conventional-looking businessman, gradually having erased the looser, more academic style to which, from my days in graduate school, I had remained habituated. Looking back now, I realized I was beginning to act conventional and stodgy, with the outer image profoundly influencing the inner man.

There was one other thing she had done, and this was perhaps of greatest importance. Early on, she began coaching me to speak in a different manner, more quickly, in a slightly higher register and with more Americanisms than I customarily used. We used a tape recorder to teach me certain effects, one of which was to achieve a more nasal sound. She also taught me to slur words, to use a more rounded R. Then, as a training measure, she would take me out and make me practice at airline counters, at the grocery store, in casual conversation with strangers, and even at client meetings. At the same time, she had me speak normally when I was with her so that the acquired speech shouldn't become habitual.

As she explained it, I was doing nothing more difficult than what a character actor does in a long-running play. I would simply be performing for two years, with my midwestern American accent constantly getting heavier, while at night, offstage with Lorraine, I would revert to my normally slower, more measured speech, which had shed most of its Americanisms during my years in Europe. She even thinned down my easy fluency in French by forcing me to acquire a more anglicized accent, and this I introduced among my francophone clients so slowly that after a time it seemed to them that I had always been guilty of anglophone distortions of their tongue. Interestingly enough, it was easier to play this kind of game in French—which was not my native tongue—than in English, since I had often in the past done my own clownish imitations of various American colleagues who proved totally unable to acquire a proper French accent.

"Now," Lorraine finally said to me, "you can remove the blinders."

I reached up and uncovered my eyes, staring straight ahead, prepared for the worst. But she had removed the mirror.

"Here," she said, from behind me.

I turned and confronted a full-length glass. The reflection it sent back startled me. I was looking at a stranger! My immediate reaction was to think that she had tricked me by putting me into a different disguise. Then, as I looked more closely, I began to notice the familiar details. The way I used to wear my hair, the way I used to wear my clothes, my shorter stature. Not only didn't I identify with what I saw, I didn't like most of it. My pants were too short. The crepe-soled shoes were a shade too informal. My jacket was too tight. My eyes had a washed-out look. I frowned, unable to believe the image I saw in front of me. I strutted back and forth, swiveling my head away and back suddenly as though to catch myself off guard.

Lorraine tittered. I turned on her. She was standing there holding a hand to her mouth, trying with difficulty to stifle further drollery.

"I can't believe it," I said.

"No, the trouble is, you do believe it. But you do not like yourself."

I nodded. "It's odd. I look out of style, inappropriate. But you know, it's mostly the clothes. You could have changed me just with the clothes."

"I believe in doing a thorough job."

"I doubt if I'll wear these clothes." I held my hands up. "They don't feel right."

"You look very nice."

"I didn't realize I was so short."

"You are not short."

"Shorter than I remember. Anyway, it's different. I mean, maybe Hightrestle won't recognize me after all."

"But you are not sure."

"No. I might look like someone else at first glance, but after a few moments, details are bound to show. He's got awfully sharp eyes, I tell you."

"Trust me. He will never know. There's no turning back now."

I rubbed a hand across my face. "I feel so naked," I confessed.

"But you won't be. Always, when I have visualized Bazenrüd, he had a beard. It is right for him, this beard. Do you not feel the same way? I need your opinion. Since you are Bazenrüd, it is for you to say if, as Bazenrüd, you feel you belong with a beard."

"Well, yes, actually. A beard would be quite the proper thing for a man like that. Adds to the mystery. But, as a practical matter, it'll take me weeks to grow a beard."

"For the present, you will use a false beard. But you must stop shaving immediately."

Then she had me sitting down while in her usual meticulous way, she fitted a large beard to my face and chin, one that was certainly the proper color but was far too big for my head.

"It has to be shaped. That's why it comes so large."

The shaping turned out to be a joint effort. As she put it, we were now working on my permanent face and she wanted me to be comfortable with it. "A beard is an important aspect of masculinity," she informed me. "You will find in time that much of your male vanity is bound up in it. So it's important that you are pleased with it."

"How can you possibly know that much about it?"

"What is it they say about not having to be a horse to judge a horse?"

"A horse race."

"Whatever. But I have much experience with horses."

"You don't have to remind me," I said.

She put down the scissors and comb. I was sitting on a stool before the small mirror, which she'd restored to the makeup table, and she was standing behind me. Now, she reached across my shoulders and took my face in both her hands, holding it tightly, while pressing her face to mine. Our images, trapped in the mirror, gazed back at each other. "*Pauvre petit,* you are jealous. That pleases me. But only from you. Besides, you must not be jealous of a past that is over."

"Over?" I repeated, feeling a sudden warm glow at her words. "Because of me?"

"Because for a long time since we have worked together, I have come to care for you very much. *Tu n'est pas comme les autres.*" Her voice, half an octave below normal, had broken into semiquavers of tenderness. I melted at the sound of it and suddenly lost all my inhibitions, turning away from the mirror to her lovely face, slowly settling my mouth on her lips, clinging to them for a long moment, to the accompaniment of mutual sighs and murmurs of endearment. In that moment, we finally and firmly established our emotional commitment to one another. But we held off any deeper consummation. The urgency of our project demanded first attention. Without saying anything more, quietly aware that something momentous had happened, we returned to styling the beard, which took another half hour before I was ready to say I was pleased with it.

Two hours later, after a phone call to Hightrestle, I was on a plane headed to Gatwick Airport, my heart still pounding. But by this time, with trepidation instead of passion, as I ventured on to my first public appearance as Bazenrüd.

Chapter Ten

Lorraine had told me that all actors experience stage fright when first appearing in a new role. But, she added, I had already played my big role and now I was merely myself. The easiest of roles. I had only to remember that and to speak and walk in my normal manner. What did it matter that I now called myself Bazenrüd instead of Horgan? Nevertheless when my cab brought me to Whitehall, my palms were wet, my eyes felt watery, and I was breathing much too fast for a man with the aplomb that Bazenrüd was supposed to possess. On the other hand, I felt somewhat protected behind my new beard. A flimsy bastion, but better than nothing.

Hightrestle, in recognizing that Edouard Bazenrüd was a very important personage, had left word for me to be ushered into his presence as soon as I arrived. So I had scarcely time to get my breath when I found myself crossing the threshold of his office. He was sitting behind his desk, which faced the door, and his piercing eyes were looking directly toward me as I entered. I felt as though I were walking into a machine gun nest.

But then, Hightrestle rose up from his seat, hurried around the end of his desk and greeted me with a strange little bow. He didn't even offer to shake my hand, as though I were too august a being to contaminate with such plebian contact. "Do please be seated, Mr. Bazenrüd."

I am not slow. I saw that I was, as they say, out in the clear and running. My confidence came flooding back. It was with an almost clownish sense of irony, as I accepted the chair he held for me, that I said: "Hightrestle, I presume?"

"Most certainly, sir." He didn't bat an eye over my salutation. "And very grateful that you took the trouble to respond to our situation, to this grave threat to the royal navy."

I was appalled and astonished. The man was positively fawning over me—me, a pure media creation, with my mysterious and puissant reputation fed by Lorraine's artful contributions. "If there's any gratitude to be expressed, you can thank Edward Horgan. He was most eloquent on your behalf. So, then—" I crossed my hands over my belly and leaned back in my chair, very conscious of the fact that instead of simply being myself, I was falling into a new role: the prescient and formidable *homme des affaires,* Edouard Bazenrüd. I noticed too that Hightrestle's eyes didn't look nearly as penetrating as they had at our earlier encounter. In fact, he seemed to have difficulty meeting my own steady Bazenrüdish gaze.

"Ah, yes," said Hightrestle, settling back behind his desk. "The Exocet missiles. They are already en route. An extremely difficult, but . . . if I may ask, how does a man of your, ah, specialized interests propose to deal with such a . . . ?" He left the question hanging in the air to speak for itself.

"My field, Hightrestle, is information." I was regurgitating Lorraine's Lesson One. "Banking, finance, manufacturing, technology, all the precincts of the modern world within which I operate depend entirely on information. Things can be made to stop and start with information. They can be pushed forward or turned around with information. Even Exocet missiles already on the way to delivery."

I was intrigued by my own eloquence, which emerged, I realized, because operating behind the personality of Bazenrüd, I had seemingly acquired new powers.

"Yes, yes, of course. But what information, may I ask?"

"The case is really very simple. Every one of those missiles was put together by means of a tightly knit chain of information. My people are already at work seeking a weak link in that chain. Indeed, as we sit here, they may already have found it."

"Yes, I'm sure. But, this particular chain of information, well, I'm only a humble civil servant, as I'm sure you'll understand . . ."

"I'm referring, of course, to the Quality Assurance chain. Without that chain, such things as missiles with their complex guidance systems, their intricate chemistry and electronic components, could never be built. At least, never more than one at a time."

Hightrestle frowned. Somehow, this didn't impress him. "Well, yes, I understand that quality control plays a major part in production, but I still don't see—"

"Not quality control," I interrupted, making my voice sound like a shout without raising it by as much as a decibel. It was a new trick of emphasis I'd acquired on the spot, another awakened Bazenrüd talent. "Quality Assurance. Capital Q, capital A. Don't you know the difference?"

I was preparing to launch into a disquisition on the subject, something that Lorraine had specifically warned me against. "In and out fast," she had admonished. "Remember, this is your first appearance. Don't get into anything where you might slip up. Just tell him that everything is under control and you can guarantee that no missiles will reach Argentina. He will take your word for it." When I'd asked why he'd take my word, she simply replied. "Because you're Bazenrüd."

And here I was, discovering that she'd been absolutely right. Yet still I felt this terrible urge to lay it all out. After having been bottled up for two years, I, Bazenrüd, couldn't resist the opportunity to flex my muscles, to try my strengths, or, just plainly, to strut my stuff. "Quality Assurance," I explained, "is the information chain that watches the production process every step of the way." I scrambled my metaphors with enthusiasm. "Nothing moves without being written down and signed according to a strict procedure laid out by the Quality Assurance manager and his team. Thus, every screw and bolt, every integrated circuit, every microchip, every movement in the assembly process exists in duplicate on paper and can be examined. The system was originally developed by the atomic energy industry in the United States, in order to guarantee the ultimate in safety. Since then, it has spread to most other production processes with remarkable results in eliminating errors, waste, and mismanagement and assuring a uniformly effective product. Do you follow me?"

"Yes, yes, but how does this stop the Exocet missiles from reaching Argentina?"

"One tiny error in the production process can turn the whole shipment around."

"But you just said that Quality Assurance prevents such errors."

"No, there are always errors. Smaller and smaller, for the most part. But Quality Assurance allows us to find and correct them."

"I still don't see how . . ."

"One single error in a missile guidance system can become a disaster for those who use such a missile, do you not agree?"

"Yes, but . . ."

"Sometimes, a very minor error is overlooked before a product goes into shipment. Nothing of consequence when we're dealing with an automobile or an electric razor. But a missile," I swiftly raised my hands and made a sound like "Poof." Followed by the single expletive: "Disaster."

"Agreed, but these investigators of yours, what if they don't find a weak link in this Quality Assurance chain?"

I shrugged. "My experience tells me, there is nearly always something. Now usually, that something is so small it will not make any practical difference. But, if attention is called to it, then the missile has to be recalled. Once there is knowledge, it cannot be allowed to pass. The Quality Assurance people will see to it. The missiles will be recalled. Failing that, the Argentines will be warned not to use this faulty batch."

"Really?"

"Absolutely."

"Why?"

"Because even though there may be no practical consequences in this case, Quality Assurance is like a religion. The QA managers will be adamant. And the company will listen, because only by rigid conformity to QA standards does it become possible to prevent a major disaster should it come along."

"And what are the chances that they'll find something?"

I made an elaborate Bazenrüd shrug. "Much better than a roll of the dice, my friend. That is the best I can offer you under the circumstances. I should have been called in earlier." All of this, I knew, was icing on the cake. But I was enjoying the game so much, I found it difficult to quit. "But at least," I added, "I will be able to let you know one way or another within—" I consulted the Rolex watch Lorraine had added to my sartorial accoutrements, "—within two hours from now." At this point, I deliberately rose to go. The move startled Hightrestle.

"You're leaving? That's it?"

"There is something else?" I said, deliberately throwing in a slight Hungarian inversion.

"Well, some sort of agreement as to terms for your services?"

I waved my hand. "As yet, I have done nothing. Within two hours, you will receive a call from my Geneva office to tell you whether we have succeeded. Should that prove to be the case, it shall have been my pleasure to serve Her Majesty, a lady I have always admired. In the meantime, Mr. Hightrestle, you had better be thinking of something else. In case we don't succeed." I condescended now by holding out my hand in farewell. I could feel him staring at the back of my head as with measured steps, I walked out of his office.

Chapter Eleven

"Alvin, Alvin, come on now. Wake up."

I opened my eyes. Kay was bending over me, a concerned look on her face. I noticed it was already daylight. Somehow, I had fallen asleep in my chair. How many hours had passed? The last I remembered was my story about Bazenrüd, with Hightrestle at Whitehall. But as I'd gone on with the story, I began to recall how my memory had gotten cloudy. I had gradually felt myself losing touch. Edward Horgan seemed to recede a great distance from me and I'd had to struggle to stay with his thoughts. And then it had apparently been too much and I had drifted off.

I explained this to Kay as I stood up, trying to stretch the stiffness from my joints. "It's as though I'm really back now," I tried to reassure her. "Funny, when I showed up here before, last night, I really didn't feel quite like myself. I mean my Alvin self. It had to come back gradually."

"I can see," she said. "Even your expression is different." Her eyes showed a hint of tears. She looked infinitely relieved.

"Now that I feel more used to being home," I continued, "it really does seem as though it had only been two days. Even if, for Edward Horgan, it spanned four years. God, I could use some coffee."

"I just made some. I figured, when you woke up, you'd want . . ." She didn't finish her sentence. She disappeared into the kitchen and returned with a hot coffee that she placed on the tray before my chair. I picked it up and, still standing, sipped at it eagerly. "Were you up all night then, waiting for me to wake up?"

"I think I dozed on the couch after watching you for an hour. Then when I noticed it was daylight, I got up, made the coffee and decided to wake you. You're feeling better now?"

"I'm fine. I'm really fine." I put the cup down and gave her a fierce hug. "I'm really back," I assured her again. "But there's more for you to hear. Much much more. Not only about Bazenrüd, but there was someone else, too. Later." I pressed a hand to my head. "I can't remember exactly who. But if I tell you from where I left off, maybe it'll come back to me. Did you have your coffee yet?"

"Oh yes. Do you remember where you left off?"

"It had something to do with what happened in Tibet. I mean, the part that's so hazy. Someone else intervened. Very important. A kind of going back and forth."

"Tibet? Did you say Tibet? You never said a word about Tibet. You were in England, with that man, Hightrestle. Where does Tibet come in?"

"Uh, not exactly Tibet. But close. In China actually, but very near the Tibetan border. Someone else took over."

"Maybe you shouldn't talk about it for a while," Kay said, looking at me with renewed concern.

"Oh, no. I'm all right. I'm just getting ahead of myself. Besides, I can't tell it anymore from Edouard's point of view. Because now, it's my memory. Almost like a dream, but a very clear one. But it happened. If it hadn't happened, Thongden would be finished."

"Finished?" she repeated. "But he is okay, though?"

"Yes, I got a message from him at Buckingham Palace." Then, at her look of increasing puzzlement, I added, "Sorry, don't mean to confuse you. I'll explain when I get to it. Do you remember where I left off?" I repeated once more. "It's kind of hazy at the moment. Wasn't Edouard in Hightrestle's office?"

"Edouard had just left Hightrestle's office. His first big trial of his new Bazenrüd personality."

I smiled in sudden recollection. I resumed my seat and started to tell her how Edouard, full of a strange kind of excitement, hurried back to Switzerland, scarcely able to wait until he could tell Lorraine the whole story. As I spoke, Kay thoughtfully provided me with a second coffee.

"What I couldn't get over was how easy it was," Edouard told Lorraine.

"Easy?" She stood against the window, the sun streaming through her hair, which formed a fine halo around her head. Backlighted thus, her expression remained hidden to him. "Do you call two years of endless effort and preparation easy? All the coaching, the planning, the information structure we had to set up, the people we had to select? That was easy? It worked because we invested great effort and planned well."

Edouard nodded. Then he sighed. He sat down on one of the conversational loveseats that faced one another perpendicular to the window where Lorraine was standing. She had just finished phoning Hightrestle to tell him that the company was planning a recall of the Exocet missiles. "Yes," he admitted to Lorraine. "I acknowledge all that. I just never thought it would go so smoothly. Or be so—exhilarating."

She came over and sat across from him. "Do you have a more comfortable feeling about yourself now?"

"Yes and no. You said I could be myself from now on. But behind this portentous Bazenrüd name, I don't feel at all like myself. I'm acting. Plain acting. And I don't know if I can go on acting indefinitely."

"But, all our lives we are acting. One role or another. Is it not better to be conscious of what we do?"

"In a philosophical sense, perhaps. But in reality, tell me, are you acting now, with me?"

"We are both within the same play. From that point of view, no. From the point of view of the author, yes."

"Then, if you are the author . . ."

"I? I am only a performer. Just like you."

"But this whole thing was your plan. Surely your play."

"I am still only a performer. You have heard of a play within a play?"

"Ah, the games Shakespeare plays. Who, then, is our Shakespeare, Lorraine?"

She shook her head and looked at him with wide sober eyes. "That is not for us to know. Until the play is over."

It was a cryptic conversation and he was to mull over it for a long time afterward. But in the meantime, things were happening. Lorraine, for one, had been wasting little time in taking advantage of Edward having at last assumed his Bazenrüd personality. As far as she was concerned, the real play was just about to begin, and so immediately, she announced, "By the way, you have an appointment tomorrow afternoon with a Mr. Cobb Urquehart."

"I do? Urquehart? Who's he? Here?"

Four questions in a row like that were some indication of his confusion. He was really still not quite sure yet of who he was or where he was supposed to be. Lorraine's answer was precise.

"The appointment is for Bazenrüd, of course. So naturally, it's over at our office. Urquehart is an American. He heads the paint division of Merle-Stonewater."

"I see," he said. An old curtain of memory lifted. Cobb Urquehart had been an Edward Horgan client some years earlier, before Merle-Stonewater paints had begun the phenomenal growth that now put them only a little behind Dupont's own giant paint division. Edward had done a small consulting job for Urquehart, who had been chief chemist at Merle-Stonewater at the time. Lorraine now told him that Urquehart was currently CEO of the company, which had doubled in size since Edward Horgan last had dealings with him.

"That means, he's really coming to see Edward Horgan, not Bazenrüd," he reminded her.

"Certainly. But since Edward Horgan was unavailable—"

He stood up suddenly and raised a hand to catch at the lower part of his beard. Lorraine smiled at the gesture. "It's still there," she said.

"I was more concerned about the man behind the beard," he admitted. He went to the window and peered out. "Aren't you rushing things a little?"

"You asked me that same question before you went to see Hightrestle."

"That was different. Urquehart knew me over a period of several months."

"And Hightrestle had eyes like lasers."

He shrugged. "But I just got back from seeing Hightrestle. I need time to catch my breath."

She returned his shrug with a very Gallic one of her own. "No, you must not pause now to back away from Bazenrüd. Or you will have to prime yourself all over again. You must keep this appointment with Urquehart. Do you not see?"

She was right, of course, and he nodded a reluctant acquiescence. "But what do I tell him about Edward Horgan?"

"I have already told him. After he contacted your office from New York, I sent him a fax explaining that for reasons of health, Mr. Horgan had chosen to withdraw from the business for an indefinite time. But due to Mr. Horgan's long working association with Bazenrüd, it has been arranged that Horgan clients be given preference over other new accounts acceptable to the Bazenrüd firm."

"My God, you did all that? You must've had it planned before I even left for England."

She shook her head. "No, it was spontaneous. After your call from Gatwick explaining what had happened with Hightrestle, I knew it was time. I sent the fax not only to Urquehart but to your entire client list. And before two hours, there was a call from Urquehart for a meeting tomorrow afternoon."

"To my office?"

"The Bazenrüd office. Your office now. In response to the fax. Evidently it is a matter of some urgency for Urquehart. He insisted on seeing you as soon as possible. So I made it tomorrow afternoon."

Edouard sat back down on one of the couches and looked at her. "Did he say what about?"

"Something to do with paint," she said.

"Of course. He's in the paint business. But what about paint?"

"He would not say over the phone, but he wanted to know if Mr. Bazenrüd was also a chemist."

"Yes?"

"I told him that was one of the things Mr. Bazenrüd and Mr. Horgan had in common."

Suddenly, he began to laugh. He crossed his hands over his abdomen and leaned back and roared. It was as though all the tension, all the pressures he'd been carrying around with him for so long now had abruptly shattered. "It's absolutely deliciously insane," he managed to exclaim between gasps of risibility. "Completely, marvelously unreal."

Lorraine, taken aback by his outburst, simply stood there with a nervous, uncomprehending expression that gradually gave way to a quiet, almost impish smile as she sensed the unexpected mood of detachment that must have seized him for just that necessary instant to permit him an altered view of the entire situation. Later, he thought of her allusion to a play within a play and realized that he had stepped back for a moment into the real play, not the one where Edward Horgan was desperately trying to relate to being Bazenrüd, but beyond both personalities, to where he himself stood, neither the one nor the other. In a flash of vision, he had seen the whole comedy, from the point of view of some mysterious other self, somehow more fundamental and less personal. And the laughter tore out of him. Then it was gone, and he heard Lorraine saying:

"Now you know."

He looked back at her, very gravely now. "For an instant," he admitted. "For an instant, I really did."

Cobb Urquehart was a big man whose rumpled suit and laid-back manner concealed an acuity that under present circumstances made Edouard uncomfortable. They were sitting in lounge chairs, facing each other across a round walnut table on which Urquehart had laid his briefcase and withdrawn a sheaf of reports. It was the room where Lorraine always met with her clients. It had deep pile carpeting and a view of Lake Geneva. The walls, papered in a gold-textured pastel green, were adorned with nicely framed sketches, two of which were Goya originals. There were some works by other artists, lesser known, but of equivalent draftsmanship. There were no phones in the room and no amenities except the sterling coffee server and accompanying bone porcelain service in an unadorned white.

"Of course, I was surprised about Ed Horgan. Never figured him as havin' a health problem." Urquehart spoke with a rural Virginia drawl, something he had never lost even after having spent the last twenty years at the Merle-Stonewater plant in eastern Massachussetts, only sixty miles from Boston. "How well did you know him, Mr. Bazenrüd?" He pronounced it Bazzinrood, the first syllable rhyming with *jazz*.

"I met him only twice, actually. But he did a lot of business with our firm through my wife."

"But you're a chemist, you say?"

"As it happens."

"Our problem, which is an urgent one," and here Urquehart shuffled a thick report lying on top of the sheaf he'd drawn from his briefcase, "calls for a spate of chemistry and a right smart source code for a very special material. Interesting that you and Ed have the same first name. Mind if I call you Ed?"

Urquehart almost seemed to be burlesquing himself. It was hard to tell whether he was seeking to draw Bazenrüd out a little more before making any commitment, or whether he already had a suspicion Bazenrüd wasn't who he was supposed to be. When he asked about calling him Ed, it was as though he not only wasn't impressed by the whole Bazenrüd façade, but he'd already spotted the real Ed Horgan hiding behind it.

"Ed? No one ever called me that, I must say."

"Never? Not even as a kid? What'd they call you in school? I understand you went to school in the good ole U.S.A."

"Aah." Edouard raised his hands diffidently. "You Americans like nicknames. They called me Bazz," he said, improvising wildly.

"Hey, I like that, Bazz." He nodded. And suddenly, he launched himself into the subject that had brought him. "This," he said, waving the report at the other, "is the result of some interesting research at Boston U chemistry department. Funded by Merle-Stonewater, I might add. Shows how adhesion qualities of polymerized paints, that includes our whole line of acrylics, show a marked increase in direct ratio to the level of uniformity—oh hell, Bazz, what it says is that when the polymer molecules are all the same size, the paint sticks better. A helluva lot better. And we've found a way to get that molecular uniformity better'n anyone else. The competition has been looking for the right monomers to help them do it. But we've found the answer in the catalysts we use in addition-polymerization. You follow me? It's the catalyst that knocks those chains into uniform molecules. One special little catalyst, and zowie, we've got a product that'll put the competition down in the basement for as long as we can keep the supply cornered. Understand? Worth millions and that's an understatement."

"And the catalyst is a secret?" Edouard asked, suddenly intrigued.

"Well, yes and no. Maybe till tomorrow, y' might say. Those boys at Dupont aren't going to be long behind us. Wouldn't surprise me none if they got one of our researchers on their own payroll. No flies on those fellows. So, no, the real secret is getting our hands on the supply. That's where you come in. At least, that's where I'd have turned to Ed Horgan with some confidence. But the word I hear around is you could maybe be a whole lot better even than Ed. Why you even look a little like old Ed. But more continental, I'd say. Is that right, Bazz?"

"Is what right?"

"That you're even better at this kind of thing than Ed."

"And the catalyst? Or do you want me to sign a nondisclosure agreement?"

"Shucks, what for? You either know a way to source the catalyst or you don't. You ain't gonna tell Dupont. Not if Ed Horgan recommended you. That's a sight better'n a disclosure agreement." He opened the report he was holding, which Edouard now observed was stamped TOP SECRET on the cover, and holding it open, swiveled it around and thrust it toward the other.

Edouard looked down and immediately caught the word printed in boldface: ADRAMACITE. For a moment, he was nonplused. Then slowly, memory followed a thin trail all the way back to his student days. Adramacite, a rare element, he couldn't recall its chemical valence, of no known practical application. Reportedly used in Africa, specifically Uganda, some thousands of years ago, where shards of pottery from an archaeological dig were discovered. Although no traces of the element were ever found through chemical analysis of the pottery, the element itself was found around the sites where the pottery was made. Of course, he realized now, with Cobb sitting in front of him: because it had probably had only a catalytic function, it wouldn't have been present at all in the artifacts.

"Uganda," Edouard said aloud.

"That's the problem," Cobb said. "Getting supplies out of that warring, messed up country, well it's just too uncertain. Can't build a business on the zigs and zags of their tribal politics. If we could, we wouldn't need you. You find us solid accessible sources and you can count on a stock deal that'll fill your heart with joy."

Edouard took a few minutes to do some research after Cobb left, and then he and Lorraine talked about it. "Now, of course, we can't send search teams all around the world looking for adramacite. And even if we did, you can be sure Dupont has the muscle to outdo us there."

"Yes?" said Lorraine. "Am I about to hear a better suggestion?"

"Well, there is a way," he admitted.

"But there's a condition?"

"Yes."

"A difficult condition?"

"I don't know. It's in your department."

"Please be more specific."

"We need access to an advanced remote sensing facility."

"I don't know what that is."

He explained to her how earth-orbiting satellites were able to gather information by means of what were known as remote sensing devices, particularly infrared and SLAR, a type of radar that could penetrate cloud cover. He then told her how those same satellites followed vertical orbits sending back a continuous stream of digitized photographs, including radar and infrared images of the ground, and further, how in the exploration for minerals, these same satellites had accumulated a body of photo signatures indicating the presence of a wide range of elements across the entire globe.

"Then, you mean," Lorraine said, "that all we have to do is look for the signature of adramacite in that photo database? And we'll know all the places adramacite can be found?"

"Not so simple," he replied. "There is no signature for adramacite."

"Why not?"

"To develop a signature, you have to verify something on the ground first and then see how it shows itself on various types of imaging sensors. No one was ever interested enough to do that for adramacite."

"Then—?"

"Well, there are very few elements likely to be found all by themselves. Usually, they turn up in combination with various other elements. Because they exist in complexes, you see? I mean, take the Ugandan site. There were fifteen other known elements also present with the adramacite. Very likely, wherever that combination of known elements can be found, there'll be adramacite."

"I see. Likely, but not guaranteed."

"Nothing's guaranteed. But, you see, all one has to do is write a simple computer program that would select from the database already accumulated within a major remote sensing center, all the places around the earth where a similar known combination exists. When we get such a selection, we go and check for the presence of adramacite."

"As simple as that?"

"Maybe. But we need one key thing. Access to a major remote sensing center database. Now, most of the developed countries have such centers. The United States has the largest. And probably I could get permission through the mining industry association to examine nonclassified data of the kind we're looking for. But since so much satellite technology in the U.S. is involved with Cold War military surveillance, it would probably take months. There's a very accessible remote sensing center in Canada where they'll gladly take you on a tour; a lot of their work is involved with geological survey and forestry and mapping, and working with the mining industry there. But I'd have to go to Canada to check it out. A week's work. On the other hand, France also has a remote sensing center which, with your connections, I'm sure you can access with just a phone call . . ."

"Aha."

"Why do you say *aha*?"

"Because I thought you did not approve of my using my French connections, as you used to call them. You are suddenly less diffident about it. Why?"

She was right, he realized. Whenever she had made use of her "connections" previously, he had felt uncomfortable and disapproving. Now, it was as though all those feelings had been wiped away. Why? As he looked at her, realizing that her face had become by now as familiar to him as his own—what was he thinking? His own? But his own face wasn't at all as familiar to him as hers. Certainly not so soon.

No, something else had changed. It was as though having cast off Edward Horgan, he had also cast off an ingrained priggishness. There was more to being Bazenrüd than a change of name. Did it have something to do with the possibility that having lost his known identity, he had lost a whole complex of attitudes that had gone into the making of it? And that as Bazenrüd, he had not so much acquired a new identity as freed himself from any and all such narrow identification? Again, he felt a renewed exhilaration. As he looked at Lorraine, he knew that whatever her past had been, it was gone for good, along with his own. Whatever belonged to his personal world was empty of yesterday's baggage. And he realized that, at this moment, Lorraine was the largest part of that personal world. "I can't really say why," he explained to her, "but somehow, what mattered to Edward Horgan doesn't seem to matter in the same way to—Bazenrüd."

Her expression was quizzical. "I'm not sure I prefer it that way," she admitted.

He shook his head. "No, no, it's because you matter more. Not less."

She turned away for a moment. "A phone call, you say. Under what government department would this remote sensing center be?"

"Whatever would fall under mining and resources, probably."

Lorraine spent the next three hours on the phone. By late afternoon, she had the information. "Nothing," she told him, throwing up her hands. "I gave them the list of all fifteen elements. They did a thorough database search. There's not another site anywhere in the world with just that combination of fifteen elements."

"Well, probably not," he admitted. "We've apparently got too many elements."

"Too many? I don't understand. You told me—"

"—that those were the elements found at the Ugandan site. Yes. But it's possible one or several of them were not essential to the presence of adramacite. In fact, I figured that might prove the case. What we have to do now is check the database for the same complex of elements, but each time, reducing the complex by one element. You see, it may be that only the presence of a few of those original fifteen elements are necessary to the presence of adramacite."

As it turned out, only five elements were needed. By mid-morning of the next day, she had found a site in China with exactly five of the elements present at the Ugandan site. The exact combination of elements did not guarantee that adramacite would be found, but it certainly increased the likelihood. Besides, he knew of no faster way to do a global search for the key element.

Chapter Twelve

*One is simultaneously less and more than his or her
former self, newly connected with the world at large
but also more powerful, independent and self-sufficient.
Such experience typically confers a confluence of freedom
and security that does not depend on this or that set
of ideas and behaviors. And it is often marked by a
coincidence of newness with something remembered.
While it lifts one beyond reminders of the ordinary
self, it is immediately recognizable, so much so that
for some people it appears to reveal their true identity
or original nature. . . .*

—Michael Murphy

Kay lay with her head resting in the corner of the couch, where the arm joined the back. Her eyes were closed but she wasn't asleep. As soon as I broke off my narrative for a prolonged moment, she opened her eyes.

"Why did you stop?"

"I thought maybe you'd fallen asleep."

"I wasn't asleep. Besides, you're kind of puzzled about something. I can tell. Your voice changed."

"Well, yes. I was trying to figure out something about Bazenrüd. When he studied the map and located the place in China, and found it was right near the Tibetan border, five hundred miles east of Lhasa, to be exact . . ."

"Yes, well?"

"Well, I wouldn't be here telling you this whole story in such detail if I hadn't somehow connected with Bazenrüd. I mean, for me, the bleedthrough only really occurred at that moment. And what I've told you so far has been a lot of clear memory. But at that juncture, when Bazenrüd found the tiny Chinese village of Hokow, the bleedthrough happened for both of us. As though the proximity of Tibet made him aware of another aspect to his mission. Almost as though he'd developed, in that moment, a kind of Alvin consciousness."

Kay shook her head. "Just like that?"

"Oh, I doubt it was just like that. Either it was part of Thongden's plan, or as Thongden had explained to me earlier, the multifaceted aspect of the event, the whole clump of organically connected purposes, came together. Just as it was meant to."

"You're trying to tell me, Bazenrüd suddenly knew about you?"

"I wouldn't call it knowing. It was more like an expansion of selfhood. A sense of being larger than one's personal identity." I threw up my hands. But the way Kay looked at me, I knew I'd have to try harder to make her understand.

"Look at it like this," I said. "The fact that a *tulpa,* a thought form, can become real and active, or even a thought form such as the Superman I imagined, or the Bruce Wayne I imagined, what does all that mean? Clearly, it says that consciousness precedes form. Otherwise, how can it have the ability to produce life in its fundamental cellular form?" As I said this, I could still see her struggling. "All right," I went on. "Think of it this way. Let's say that consciousness imagines a something, *A*, which produces a something *B*, which produces *A* again. What I'm saying is that consciousness, through imagination, apparently can produce form. Just form. An outline, a boundary. But form cannot exist as an emptiness. Something rushes in to fill it. An identity. An Alvin. Or a Bazenrüd.

"But not just a simple and pure identity. The Alvin identity, as we know, has all sorts of fragmentary identities clinging to it, like a Superman phantasm or a Batman phantasm. And as to that, we each have dozens of phantasms of all the other boundary forms our consciousness has created, some stronger, some weaker, depending on many things. And sometimes there are these bleedthroughs, so that the boundaries blur into each other. Like Alvin blurring into Bazenrüd, and Bazenrüd blurring into Alvin, and God knows how many other fragmentary personalities we've got bobbing around to make us the way we are. We're one and many at the same time."

Again I raised my hands in a way meant to suggest I had reached the limit of my capacity to explain it. "So somehow, the Tibetan-Chinese link connected us at that point, and Bazenrüd became aware of Alvin in some way, just as I did of him. But as he might have put it himself, he was onstage in this particular act. It was his job to get the adramacite, which would set in motion all the things that were also important to me, and to Thongden. Do you see?"

Kay was quiet for a while. She bent forward on the couch and cupped her chin in her hands. "I think so. In a dim sort of way, yes."

"I don't think I can make it clearer with words alone. But the way things happened from that point on, that should illustrate it much more sharply."

"And what happened?"

"Okay," I said. "Let me sort it out. First, the potential adramacite deposit was somewhere near that village of Hokow. In Xinkang Province. A place, if it helps any, about two hundred miles west of the capital of Szechuan Province, Changdu. I mention it because Sze-chuan is a more familiar place-name historically, the province where Mao staged his great retreat and built the movement that was later to overthrow the Kuomintang. And invade Tibet. Anyway, Hokow itself lies in the foothills of one of the highest peaks in the Himalayan chain. Seven thousand, five hundred ninety meters, or twenty-four thousand, nine hundred feet. The remote sensing data showed the mineral deposit somewhere high up on the eastern flank. And as in all remote sensing operations, it would require the final confirmation of a ground expedition. That's when things began to get interesting."

I went on to explain how Bazenrüd immediately contacted the Swiss office of an official export company of the People's Republic of China, for whom he had performed a number of services in the recent past. Could they secure a permit for Bazenrüd's team to explore for adramacite on the flanks of Minya Konka? Naturally, the People's Republic would be sure to realize a substantial royalty in hard currency on any subsequent export of the material.

Normally, Bazenrüd might have expected an answer in about two weeks, since the bureaucracy of the PRC did not exactly oper-ate at Western levels of efficiency. But to his surprise, the answer came within two days. To his even greater surprise, it consisted of an emphatic and unqualified *No*.

"That means only one thing," Bazenrüd told Lorraine when the fax arrived from the PRC export company's Geneva office.

Lorraine nodded. "Something else is going on there that they don't want you to see."

"Not me, or anyone else," Edouard admitted. He was seated at the little conversational table, studying the fax. Lorraine sat across from him. Outside, it was a serene day, offering a beautiful, clear view of the mountains beyond the city.

Lorraine, who had been watching him closely, noted something in his expression that startled her. "What is it?" she asked. "You have the look of—I cannot say, but as though for a moment, I did not know you."

He nodded in agreement, somewhat surprised at himself, as he said, "I—yes, for a moment, I didn't know what was happening. A sudden pressure, a certainty. Or, maybe a very strong hunch? But I had this strange feeling that came from very deep, a part of me I'm not always aware of, and it seemed to be telling me that now—*it's happening.*"

Lorraine frowned. "What is happening?"

"That they would deny me . . . we've been on such good terms. As though something else interfered. Something they may have lost control of."

"I do not know what you are talking about, Edouard." She always called him Edouard now. Never Edward, since the transformation.

He leaned toward her. "Our real reason. The purpose behind what we are doing. It has just presented itself."

She paled. "How can you know that?"

Always articulate, he now dropped into French as though to help himself search for the words he couldn't find in English. "It has to do with the meaning of their refusal. They would not ordinarily refuse me. But it suddenly came to me. There is something I must not be allowed to see. Something in Minya Konka. Suddenly, the fact that I need to go to that particular place . . ." He broke off and shook his head and resumed in English. "No, I am not explaining it properly. Let me put it this way. When the news came that they would not let me in, I had this certainty. But it wasn't I, Edward Horgan, or Edouard Bazenrüd, that had that certainty. For a moment, I was yet another. Someone else." He threw up his hands. "I really can't explain it. Maybe, after a while, it will get clearer. All I can say is, that other self was there just long enough to understand that the reason behind the refusal was something dark. Very dark indeed. The very darkness that we have been building up all our strength for. Does that make sense to you?"

"I'm not sure," she said falteringly. "Except that I knew it would come like this. Only I thought I would be the one."

He looked at her strangely. "I even think," he said surprisingly, "that you do know. That precisely because you know, you have closed it off. You do not like what it means."

"What are you saying?"

"Because of what it requires," he said. "That's not easy for you."

"And what is that, Edouard?"

"That I must go there, to Minya Konka, myself."

"No," she said between compressed lips. "I do not think so."

"And if I don't," he went on relentlessly, "then everything we have been trying to get ready for, all of it, has been wasted. Do you understand that?"

She looked at him with a concern he had never seen in her before. "And you propose to go, without permission?"

"Because they refused permission."

"The adramacite is not that important," she said. "Not to us."

"You know very well it's not a matter of adramacite. But finding it will uncover something more important."

"You don't know what?"

"I only have this powerful feeling, that it's extremely important. But I don't know why."

She thrust her clasped hands toward him in that characteristic way. "Sometimes such feelings are not what they appear to be. They are not always accurate. Sometimes, we have these, what you might call, stumblings of the psyche." She was arguing hard against him now.

Suddenly he smiled at her. "Ah, how well I know you," he said. "You are dissembling. You're determined to protect me."

She shook her head. "You are talking about something very dangerous. That is not your—your forte, Edouard."

"Nevertheless, I feel equal to it. In any case, the need to go is very strong. You must understand that."

"If I say no, will you go anyway?"

He nodded. "I must go."

She stared out the window, squinting into the brightness of the day. "I will never say no to you. But, I will insist that you take Jean-Marc with you. It is more—"

Bazenrüd smiled. "I know, *his* forte. But . . . I don't feel right about asking him to take the risk."

"He will feel hurt if you venture into something like this without him. Besides, he has a knowledge of Mandarin. Because you need him, I will insist on this one concession."

After a moment of reflective silence, she added, "You will have to slip in illegally and then work your way across thousands of miles of rugged and desolate terrain. You propose to do that, yet a little while ago, you did not want to take the trouble to wait one week to get information on adramacite from the Canadian Remote Sensing Center. I do not understand your motive."

Edouard stroked his hand downward along his beard. "I can't say, really. It has something to do with what I am, I mean since I became Bazenrüd. When personalities can be cast off and changed like a suit, you begin to get a sense of being something more. Something—" He shook his head. "I don't know. Of being really somebody much more than I ever suspected. And then, well, in this case anyway, it creates a pressure to do this particular thing. A deeper voice speaking in me, you might say. All I know is, that the intellect by itself is only a kind of steering mechanism. A small thing. It cannot help us in the larger decisions. It can only be useful for carrying out a decision that comes from somewhere else."

She seemed moody as she heard him out. She sat down, staring at the floor. "I have sometimes gotten such a feeling," she admitted, "when I had to throw myself into a very difficult acting role. But," she gazed up at him, "I never had such an impulse to throw myself into so dangerous an undertaking. How will you ever manage it?"

Edouard shrugged. "With your help."

"My help?"

"Your insistence that I take Jean-Marc with me, for one thing. I realize, of course, that could make all the difference. Together, he and I will figure a way."

"What we have to do," Jean-Marc said, placing a stubby index finger on the map, "is enter through Nepal. In the Khumbu, the region closest to Everest, we can discuss our problem with some of the Sherpas. As you know, most of them speak English, since they have been working many years now for all the European trekkers requiring guides for an Everest climb."

"Our problem in what sense?" Edouard said.

"Our problem is getting around from just south of Everest and finding a route northward to the Brahmaputra River. Which, as it passes through Tibet, is known also as the Huang Po. It appears easier to make that northward trek if we strike out from a point in Khumbu, although the route from there to here . . ." and again his finger followed the sinuous passage of the river as it passed Lhasa, continued on for another hundred or so miles and then, taking a tremendous bend, turned south. That bend was precisely the point he indicated. "This will get us only so far. Navigating downriver to this point will then require an overland trek through difficult mountain terrain to here," and his finger pointed to an obscure spot on the map somewhat further east. "This will be Dango Gompa. We can rest here and see what preparations we can make to continue on to Minya Konka, where the going will be along narrow mountain trails, threatened by avalanches and rock slides as well as the most treacherous weather you can imagine." He paused and looked up at Edouard. "For an experienced mountaineer, it would be a difficult journey, but possible. For you—well, to put it bluntly, you are not in shape for it."

"You're saying then that this route is impossible for me and that I'd have a better chance by flying directly to Changdu and then heading east to Minya Konka, even though I'm almost sure to be detected by the Chinese?"

"We would have to fake an entrance permit to get you into Changdu, of course."

"Still, the Han Chinese would know I was there. They would be watching for me, now that they know I'm interested. Whatever they're hiding at Minya Konka will be very well guarded around a very broad periphery."

"True. Either choice you make offers a high probability of failure."

"You speak of probabilities, Jean-Marc. But there is something you have not said."

Jean-Marc nodded. "If we can get you to Dango Gompa, well, you understand that this is a monastery of the fabled Yellow Hat sect. It is possible that they would have ways of getting to Minya Konka that the outside world knows little about. But," and here Jean-Marc raised his hands in a gesture of uncertainty. "But, whether it is something that you can make use of, I cannot say. This much, let me add. The way through Changdu is hopeless. The way through Dango Gompa offers a slight possibility. Very slight. It would almost seem that you should not go at all."

"I would like to know more about that very slight thing you refer to."

Again that shrug from Jean-Marc. "I really cannot say. I remember only that the monks in those mountainous fastnesses had some strange ways of getting around. Things they had been learning for perhaps centuries about the sheer physics of movement and energy. Or they could not have survived, themselves. My mother used to tell me about unusual methods of walking, of secret disciplines that helped store vast reserves of energy. For the rest, it is likely that among the Sherpas, somewhere, we will find someone who can tell us more about it. Myself, as I look at the possibilities, I do not think you should go. You will die there."

But Edouard was convinced that he knew something he could not have communicated to Jean-Marc. "We will go, nonetheless," he said quietly.

Chapter Thirteen

*We were creatures of many different dimensions
passing through each other's lives like ghosts through
doors. Our identity is a dream. We are process, not
reality, for reality is an illusion of the daylight, the light
of our particular day.*

—LOREN EISELEY

*Unknown to us, hidden aspects of the self look after us
and shoulder part of the load. . . . Many contemporary
researchers believe these multiple, hidden parts of
ourselves may play a key role in creativity, healing and
other exceptional abilities.*

—LARRY DOSSEY, M.D.

The man they needed to see was a well-to-do Sherpa guide named Lobsang Tsienpu. According to Jean-Marc, they would have to find him somewhere around the nearest takeoff point for Everest. The reason they would find him here had to do with the nearly century-old interplay between the European and Himalayan cultures. Starting around the early 1900s, avid mountain climbers from the west began to arrive among the local Sherpa population, which consisted of some thirty-five thousand very traditional Buddhists, most of whom represented a spillover directly from Tibet. These Nepalese locals were never themselves interested in challenging the giant peaks they lived beneath, since they regarded them as centers of holiness. However, they were soon overwhelmed by the increasing numbers of Europeans bringing elements of European culture, the English language, and a kind of general European lifestyle to an ethnic culture that differed little from the ancient ways of their Tibetan cousins.

Within a generation, the Sherpas, with their ability to function in high altitudes, their fascination with occidental ways, and the comparative wealth that came with it, became the guides and porters of the ever-growing number of European climbers. Yet despite a superficial Europeanization, the Sherpas managed to cling to much of their ancient culture and their religious roots. Lobsang Tsienpu, himself now a little too old to be climbing peaks like Everest, had nevertheless set up a guide service in Khumbu, some miles to the east of Kathmandu and the region from which all Everest expeditions began.

"This man, Lobsang, with whom I spoke by telephone, is not only a well-to-do provider of services to the Europeans, but from what I understand, is deeply involved in the movement among the Sherpas to maintain their traditional values. He is one, therefore, who I think will understand the special significance of your mission—"

"Do you understand it, Jean-Marc?" Edouard broke in suddenly.

For some moments, Jean-Marc was thoughtful. "Understanding does not come into it," he said at last. "But I have met before certain people who have experienced a thing that, how shall I express it, surpasses their outward personality. As though they knew they were more than they seemed. This change of yours from Edward Horgan, that is only part of it. Since I have never experienced it, I cannot altogether say what it is. But I recognize it when I see it. As I recognized it long ago in Madame Lorraine."

"You—did that?"

"From the day I first understood that what she meant by theater had little to do with the literal theater."

Edouard nodded. "I see now why she insisted that you accompany me. You may understand it better than I do. But this expedition, that's what it has come to mean to me: the possibility of understanding it."

"We will go first to Kathmandu. After that," Jean-Marc said, pointing to the map, "we will take a small plane to—here."

The airport at Lukla was on a plateau 9,400 feet above sea level. It was as close as one could get by air to Khumbu some twenty miles to the north. But it was at Lukla that Lobsang Tsienpu was waiting for them. The commercialization of this remote Nepalese village astonished Edouard. The first thing he noticed was the professionally lettered English sign pointing the way to the Sherpa Coffee Shop. A short distance beyond was the low airport building, surrounded by heaps of recently cleared snow. Inside there were Sherpa women selling imitation Tibetan jewelry and other curios made in small plants in Kathmandu.

It was spring and business was brisk, with large groups of eager trekkers already crowding the vendors' stands, people from all over Europe and North America who were constantly arriving to take up the challenge of Everest. The *lingua franca* was not, of course, the Tibetan dialect spoken by the Sherpas, but English.

The man Lobsang Tsienpu, who met them in the doorway of the Sherpa Coffee Shop, was not exactly what Edouard had been expecting. He was a small man, somewhat past fifty, wearing a down-filled, fur-collared jacket and a pair of torn, padded pants tucked into low boots. But in his eyes, which peered up behind a pair of heavy lids, Edouard caught a momentary scintillation that rose unexpectedly, then dropped away behind a quiet staring opacity, as though, somehow, the Sherpa had subjected him to an instantaneous scan that reached to his very soul.

"You are not a climber," Lobsang Tsienpu said in a musical but largely British English as he reached out and grasped Edouard's outstretched hand. "But you are going on a difficult journey."

"Jean-Marc told you?"

The Sherpa lifted his hands and walked alongside Edouard as a waiter led them to a wooden table near the window, from which a view of Everest's formidable north slope was visible. "You are clearly not in shape for a serious ascent. But the look of determination, I've seen it only on the faces of the most avid climbers. You are here, I think, to accomplish something perhaps more momentous than scaling a mountain?" He turned suddenly to Jean-Marc and added something in the Mandarin dialect.

Jean-Marc nodded his head. He turned to Edouard with a wry expression. "He said," Jean-Marc explained, "that in the West there is the firmly held belief that one man can save the world. He said you strike him as perhaps being such a man."

Edouard smiled suddenly. "But I am not one man," he said.

The Sherpa looked at him in silence. Finally, he said, "It is strange to hear that from a Westerner. You see yourself, then, as an accidental—" he paused, frowned, and seemed to search for a word, as though, despite his passable fluency in English, he had never used it for this kind of conversation, "—conglomeration, yes, of energies? Not permanent?"

"That is a Buddhist notion, according to what I read. But no, I don't say that. I'm not sure yet that I can say anything, but I'm beginning to believe that I am a much larger unity than I ever imagined. Without some awareness of that, I don't think I'd even be here."

Jean-Marc went into a careful recital in Mandarin as Tsienpu listened, nodded, then turned a gaze full of curiosity on Edouard. But he remained silent.

"Good Lord," Edouard said. "He must have told you that I'm not superhuman or—" He broke off and gazed at Jean-Marc.

"I told him you were a man of great force," Jean-Marc explained.

"Well, hardly that. But I'm beginning to learn how to borrow force, when necessary." His enigmatic comment puzzled the other two.

"It is better, I think," the Sherpa said, somewhat disconcerted, "that I should start by asking how I might help you?"

Jean-Marc nodded. He reached inside his jacket and produced a map, which he unfolded and spread over the table, moving from his seat to stand alongside the guide as he explained once more in halting Mandarin. He traced a series of alternate routes with his fingers, ending up each time at Minya Konka. "That is our destination," he finished in English. "There are these various ways to get there. Some shorter. Some longer. Because it is likely that the Chinese will be watching for us. In fact, it is certain. Therefore, we must travel a route perhaps less convenient than normal to reach our destination."

"Ah-h-hh," Lobsang Tsienpu said, nodding and interlacing his fingers. "In that case, yes, yes. There is nothing for it then. To avoid the Han Chinese who have eyes everywhere along the standard routes, the longest way you have chosen is indeed the best." His fingers descended to the map. "You must go west from here, then north by way of the River Modi. It will carry you through the lower ranges of the mountain, but it will not always be navigable. Then, overland about twenty-five kilometers to the great Brahmaputra River, as it flows east. That will take you through Lhasa." He looked up from the map and fixed his eyes on each man alternately. "I am sure that you can manage the very difficult journey, to this point."

He nodded at Jean-Marc as he indicated a cross on the map where the Brahmaputra suddenly turned south. "Here, you must abandon the river and go straight east to the monastery, Dango Gompa. But as matters now stand, it strikes me that only you can make it," he repeated, indicating Jean-Marc. "This one," he pointed to Edouard, "for him, it would be impossible. Not without careful preparation. Exercises. Endurance training."

"How long?" Jean-Marc said.

"Three months. Very hard workouts. Until just at the end of the monsoons when the hundred-and-fifty-kilometer winds ripping across the high plateaus will begin to die down."

"That sounds sensible to me," Edouard agreed. "I know I need to be in better shape," he admitted. "Of course, I never realized—"

The Sherpa held up a hand. "There is more. Between the monastery here and Minya Konka, only a short distance compared to the rest—"

"Well?"

The Sherpa shrugged. "The way is impassible. Even for me."

"But then, why do you suggest such a route?" Jean-Marc said, puzzled.

A frown wrinkled the Sherpa's forehead. "There is something I cannot speak clearly about," he said, strangely echoing Jean-Marc's earlier comment. "But it has something to do with," he pointed at Edouard, "that look I noticed before." Turning to Jean-Marc, he added, "There is something about your companion that might make a difference if you can manage to get him to the monastery."

Jean-Marc nodded. His insight had been confirmed. He smiled with satisfaction.

"What do you mean?" Edouard broke in.

"The monks will also see what I see," Lobsang replied evasively.

"You will have to do better than that," Edouard pressed.

"Some of those monks are familiar with a way to travel that is very different than the ordinary means. I do not think I can explain more."

The two Westerners exchanged glances. Then Edouard said to Jean-Marc. "You mentioned this too, before we set out."

"I remembered it from things my mother told me many years before. There are many stories about this special way of traveling. Even in the west, from the German Buddhist who took the name of Lama Govinda. From that remarkable Englishwoman, Alexandra David-Neel. It is called *lon-gompa,* trance-walking."

"When do we begin training?" Edouard said, suddenly evincing no further curiosity. He would discover what was necessary in due course.

"We must start today. There's little enough time," the Sherpa said.

Edouard shrugged. "We have all the time there is," he said, with a strange half smile.

Chapter Fourteen

"**D**o you understand, then, what was happening to him?" I
asked.

Kay had moved to a more upright position on the
couch, her feet planted on the floor, her chin cupped in her hands.
"You keep intimating something." She frowned. "But, no. What was
happening?"

"Let's start with what we believe. Which is, that life takes place in
a present that stands directly between the past and future. Wouldn't
you agree?"

"Well, of course."

"But it's wrong."

"Oh?"

"Because it's only partly true. It isn't true in childhood. Or in
dreams. Or in old age. In all those states, we're not always clear
about whether it's a so-called past or a future or even a now we're
living in. The case is obvious in dreams. But think back if you can to
when you were very little, say about five."

"I can't remember anything from that far back. Not like you. But
you're not typical."

"You know," I said as a new realization struck me. "I always insisted I remembered those childhood episodes, like watching the figures on my bedroom curtains come alive, while I entered into the life I created. But after my experiences with alternate identities and parallel lives, not just Horgan and Bazenrüd, or even my abortive participation in the life of my own version of Batman, because there was also that constant breaking down of my Alvin identity all through those years I was away in the Himalayas—because for me, they were years—" I interrupted myself, realizing that I had been running on at her with a series of swift disconnected thoughts. I must have looked strange to her, judging by her puzzled expression. She raised her head and waited for me to continue.

"Yes," I said. "In those extreme and terrible situations I encountered, I had help. Flashes of insight. Surges of strength. Things that didn't come from me alone."

"Which you? Alvin or Edouard?"

I shook my head. "The strange part is, in some way, I was always present as Alvin. It was always there, lurking in the background. No matter what other identity I was acting out of. Maybe what I'm trying to express is the realization that the particular is all. That the infinite, all the possible and probable selves I am on the one hand, depends in the end on my particularity, on my being Alvin. Why? I'm not quite sure. Maybe it's why there are no two snowflakes alike. I don't believe there are any two things in the universe alike, actually. Because the Universal Spirit, or the Creator, or God or however you want to refer to that Total Ineffability, couldn't be infinite without also being totally and absolutely finite. That's why Alvin was never lost. Never during the whole time. You understand?"

"But those other selves you became? What about their—particularity?"

I held my hands out to my sides with the fingers partly curled, a gesture meant to suggest my limitation of thought. "I don't know.

Except it had to be there. Because it was theirs. I could never intrude on it. That's what I know now. That's what I suddenly realize. Without it, the notion of the infinite doesn't even make sense."

"I think," Kay said, in a quiet, almost a new, voice, "that makes me feel a whole lot easier."

"It does me too," I said, sitting down alongside her on the couch. "But I wouldn't have brought it up except for what happened. You need to know these things if you're not going to get swept into a kind of mental numbness. I mean, that our own private reality, my Alvinhood, is permanent. That you'd have to erase the whole universe just to reverse one particular like you or me. On a certain level, even a snowflake is—indelible."

"It all sounds wonderful. It's a soothing thought. Even though it's so strange."

"It gets stranger still. And it all started only a week after I'd begun my exercises with Lobsang Tsienpu."

Chapter Fifteen

At first, Lobsang put Edouard through a very prosaic routine of setting up exercises, running in place, rope climbing, push-ups, workouts on the parallel bars, in a small local gym patronized by climbers trying to shape up for the Everest challenge. Gradually, the methods changed to stretching, bending, and finally breathing, essentially hatha yoga techniques. But these did not take place in the gym; they went on in a special room in Lobsang's home.

The Sherpa lived alone. Apart from his tourist guide business, he had long ago chosen a monkish, solitary existence in which meditation played a central role. It was in Lobsang's meditation room that Edouard continued his training. Except for a typical Buddhist altar at one end, the rather small room boasted no furnishings except for a few small, scattered cushions.

Eastern light, magnified by reflections from the snow that covered the outside world, cut sharply through the monkish cubicle of a room from a single tall, wide window built into one wall. Lobsang appeared to Edouard as a blackened silhouette against the scintillating whiteness of the outside as he sat in lotus fashion just in front of the window. This was on a cloudy day when any prismatic reflections from the rising sun's direct rays were not present. Then the breathing began and Edouard, sedulously following his mentor's instructions, found himself slipping into a state unlike anything he had ever experienced before. Using one of the many variations of *nadi-sudi* known in that part of the world, Lobsang had led Edouard into a kind of self-partitioning in which, at first, it seemed as though he were separating into his two primary essences, so that he seemed to be in two places at once.

Sitting on a cushion on the floor was Edouard Bazenrüd. Standing and watching him from a place alongside Lobsang was Edward Horgan. But this impression was only momentary. From where he stood alongside Lobsang, he now seemed to see both Horgan and Bazenrüd as one entity sitting on the cushion. The entity who was watching this pair was neither. It was no more than an essential other, a pure watcher, an identity that was conscious only of its otherhood but not of itself. Not a real self but a shell of one, into which, as Lobsang was later to explain, when conditions on the trip might become so unbearable, Edouard could retreat and somehow survive.

"I don't understand how such a thing is possible," Edouard remarked one morning to Lobsang.

"In the high altitudes, you will experience a blurring of your mental faculties," Lobsang began. "There is even sometimes a mixing of identities. Mysterious selves shaped from random concatenations of thought," he went on, struggling with his British English, "will arise and take possession of your being. For us, meditation provides an antidote. For cultivated Westerners like yourself, some lifetime immersion in art and literature provides the imaginative power to endure the daily ambiguities and paradoxes, along with the tragedies, failures, and disappointments we all endure. We learn, through these arts of the imagination, to be alone with ourselves so that our essential hidden strength can hold us together in some sort of firm identity. It's what keeps us from falling apart. I believe it's what you Westerners call *character*."

It was the longest speech the Sherpa had ever made to Edouard, but it had the effect of a profound reassurance. Edouard redoubled his efforts for the balance of his training.

As it turned out, the weather favored them. The monsoons ended early that season, and they managed to set out almost two weeks earlier than they had hoped. Lobsang also brought along a pair of younger, more agile Sherpas as he proceeded to guide them first westward to the River Modi. Their route was along a high plateau whose altitude, while not nearly approaching that of Everest, was still at an elevation that would have been difficult for Edouard except for the training and especially the breathing exercises. But they still had to proceed more slowly than Edouard would have liked.

The awesome scenery, the polyform glacial mass of the smaller mountains, with their vast crevasses and their sudden puffs of distant cloud as an avalanche rumbled down their flanks, offered to Edouard the detached and cruel beauty of a nature that burned its significance into his soul, so that he sensed more strongly than ever his participation in a reality that reached far beyond his private self. In an odd way, it also seemed to bless his mission, whose mysterious necessity took on a kind of universal aspect shared by the multitude of smaller identities of which the original Edward Horgan formed a single particle and over all of which was a concise consciousness that, at the proper time, after it had all passed, he would recognize as his indestructible and private Alvin persona.

They reached the Modi River with great effort and little incident, launched their big inflatable raft upon its churning surface, with the two younger Sherpas adroitly guiding them over and around obstacles and unexpected waterfalls, floating ice chunks and the occasional blinding snow gusts. From time to time, they came to places where the river narrowed or choked with ice, becoming unnavigable, and they were forced to carry their raft on their shoulders until they could once again re-enter the capricious waters. At night, they bivouacked in portable tents whose double lining preserved their body heat against the vicious nocturnal cold. Until finally, a day came on which the world seemed to consist of implacable glacial formations locked around the lashing, aberrant waters on whose current they moved. Lobsang announced in Mandarin to Jean-Marc, "We are now inside Tibet."

Jean-Marc translated for Edouard's benefit.

"Just like that?" Edouard murmured, looking around and seeing nothing changed, since nature maintained her austere innocence of man-made boundaries.

"The trek will now be overland to the Brahmaputra, which the Tibetans call the Huang Po. We will dismantle and carry the boat to that point, a distance of perhaps thirty kilometers," Lobsang explained.

Edouard looked toward the craggy and frigid landscape that lay ahead. "It doesn't look too friendly," he remarked.

The Sherpa grinned through the breath-steamed aperture of his fur hood.

"No worse than the trails we have already mastered. But there may be troubles of a different kind."

"Yes?"

"Have you not noticed the others traveling in the opposite direction?"

Edouard realized he had been so fixated on the overwhelming landscape, that humans had appeared somehow too small, too disproportionate in scale to be noticed, so that, while he had indeed been aware of occasional parties of travelers following the path back to Nepal, he hadn't paid any particular attention to them. But now he became more observant. That very afternoon, as they struggled northward, he watched a group approaching from about two kilometers away, their figures black and unambiguous against the snowy background of the mountains.

As they drew closer, he could make them out more distinctly: a couple with two small children, an elderly man, and an elderly woman being pulled along on a crude sled consisting of bits of board covered with yak hide and lashed together with hide strips. The old woman's long white hair had slithered out through the side of the heavy fur cap she wore and trailed limply along on the icy path. What most struck Edouard was the look of fear on their faces as they drew closer, nervously slowing their approach. And then, more troubling details became apparent as Edouard noted the pinched, starved faces, the ragged anoraks, and the tattered and inadequate footwear, as though they had fled with the barest minimum of possessions and went on in a state of constant terror.

One of the Sherpas spoke to them, reassuring them with explanations that the Bazenrüd party was not Chinese, not soldiers. "Friends," he told them, using the Han Chinese word *guan-xi,* which means literally, someone intimate, someone close and personal—expressing, in those special circumstances, not only a sympathy for their plight but a partisan unity against a common enemy.

"Already two of them have died on the trail," the Sherpa explained to Edouard in English.

"See that they have enough food for the rest of the way," Edouard said.

"Perhaps too, we could spare them some warm clothing," Jean-Marc added, noting the tattered condition of their garments. The old man and the younger woman were already blue with cold.

"There will be many others," the Sherpa warned. "We cannot help them all."

Edouard nodded in agreement, then added, "But these were sent to us."

Later, after resuming their trek, Edouard said to Lobsang, "I thought the Han Chinese had agreed to relax their control of Tibet."

"Every time they rotate their military commissars, the new one tries to make his authority felt. Especially in Lhasa. But all these refugees, they are our protection."

"Why is that?"

"Because we are going in the opposite direction. The Chinese are trying to keep the people from fleeing. So since we are heading toward Lhasa, they will pay no attention to us."

"Until we get past," the youngest of the Sherpas added. "Anyone going away from Lhasa, even toward the east, toward the Chinese border, is presumed to be fleeing."

"At least," Jean-Marc said, "we can relax until Lhasa then."

Ardong, the younger Sherpa, made a movement that brought his heavy fur hood around as he gestured a forceful negative. "Not possible. Always there will be soldiers who will stop anyone. Just to exercise authority. Not so often for us, perhaps. But we must be on guard."

They continued on their way for the rest of the day, following a narrow icy trail packed down by previous travelers, almost all of whom would have been refugees moving in a southerly direction. But the next morning, after an hour of picking their way along what seemed a very gradual ascent, Lobsang, in the lead, called a halt. He pointed to several sets of footprints in the snow at the outer edges of the trail.

He spoke slowly to Jean-Marc in his little-used Mandarin.

"He's telling me," Jean-Marc relayed to Edouard, "that these were made by soldiers. Going south, probably in pursuit of refugees. They passed yesterday. It's likely they have picked up that group we assisted. The clothing we gave them would reveal that we are *pilings*—foreigners—with no legitimate business in Lhasa. By now, the patrol could be heading back to check us out. We must move as quickly as possible and keep an eye out behind us."

This was followed by another exchange between Jean-Marc and Lobsang. Again Jean-Marc turned to Edouard. "He says we must try to move faster to keep ahead of the soldiers. But we are still ascending. At this altitude, if we overstrain ourselves, some of us will suffer the effects of oxygen depletion. So Lobsang wants you and me, who are not experienced mountaineers, to wear the oxygen masks we brought along."

Ardong had already unfastened a rather large backpack carried by the tallest Sherpa among them, a man much stronger than his companions. Edouard had wondered what was in that oversized pack, but in the other distractions and excitements of the journey, he had neglected to ask. Now he knew. There was lightweight oxygen gear, consisting of fine rubberized helmets and small refillable tanks, much like a diver's gear but stripped of the excess weight that went with underwater buoyancy. Nevertheless, the equipment seemed to Edouard an unnecessary addition to the rigors of the trip.

"I don't think so," he said, waving Ardong off. He looked at Jean-Marc. "Are you going to let them encumber you with that rig?"

The former stuntman, who was still clearly in very good shape, nodded a brisk affirmative. "Neither you nor I have the breathing skills to rush ahead on these heights like our friends the Sherpas. Of course I'm going to wear mine. And I insist that you do the same. Don't be fooled by the recent training you got from Lobsang Tsienpu. Unassisted, you're not up to the speed we'll have to make at this altitude, believe me."

Edouard looked dubiously at the helmet-and-tank contraption. Ardong was patiently waiting to help him on with it. But Edouard shook his head. To Jean-Marc, he said, "You're probably correct. But why right now? I'm feeling fine. I agree that if I begin to feel the strain, I'll put the thing on."

Jean-Marc, who had by now acquired a multitude of ways to express himself silently to his friend, gave Edouard a scrutinizing look suggesting that the other's attitude might already be signaling the onset of altitude sickness. But Edouard again shook his head. "I'll know when I need it," he insisted.

With a shrug, Jean-Marc gave in and allowed Ardong to help him on with his own oxygen support. In moments, they were back on the trail, but this time they were moving much more quickly. It was necessary to put as much ground between themselves and any possible pursuers before dark, when they would have to make camp.

The weather continued mild, but by late afternoon it was growing colder as the shadows deepened in the icy canyons. They had ascended at least another nine hundred meters. Edouard, whom everyone had watched carefully for the first few hours, seemed to be bearing up surprisingly well. So the others in the party gradually withdrew their attention from him.

That was precisely when the altitude began to take its toll. Edouard was not entirely aware of what was happening, nor did anyone notice at first when his steps faltered, as though he could not find the path. It took him some moments to realize that he was experiencing the vertigo common to the onset of hypoxia. At first, he stubbornly resisted and fell slightly behind the others without saying anything. But soon, he swerved to one side of the trail and selected a low seat from among the glacial boulders that lay scattered along the way. He could feel his accelerated heart rate, was aware that he was breathing harder and faster and that he was no longer quite sure what he was doing there. He could now see the others coming toward him with anxious expressions, but he appeared to know only one of them, Jean-Marc.

He made an effort to stand, but instead, seemed to fall away from everything. He could sense that the old points of reference, the signposts, the path itself, were breaking up. All the little bends and twists, the sharp edges, the comfortable crevices from which he could always seize and renew his acquaintance with himself, were changing shape. In moments, every familiar landmark was gone, leaving memory with nothing to cling to. There was just a random massing of events, like the faces of strangers in a crowd.

"This story?" the small boy repeated. "No, daddy, not this one. Keep going."

Edward Horgan was sitting on the porch of his home in southern Vermont turning the pages of a comic book with his small son, Jack. There was no Edouard Bazenrüd, no Lorraine, not even an office in Switzerland. Not yet.

"This one." The boy, barely six years old, pointed to a page his father was about to pass. Jack had already begun learning to read, but the Batman comic was still too difficult for him.

"I read you this one just the other day."

"I want to hear it again," Jack said. "'Specially where the Batman slides down to get the bad guys shooting at him from there." His small stubby finger picked out a section of the gaudy page.

"Here, where he swings down on a rope and sweeps the three crooks off the ledge? Where he kills them? You really like that?"

The boy nodded. "I want to hear it again."

"Strange," Horgan said to the boy. "It's kind of brutal. In fact, I don't think I ever saw Batman kill anybody like that before. Doesn't seem he would do such a thing."

The boy nodded. "The crooks were shooting at him."

"I know, but—"

"Please read it."

Edward, reluctant to play the censor with this child whose mother's death two years earlier had forged a tighter bond between him and the youngster than he'd ever imagined possible, began reading. It was a story of a mysterious crime, committed by mysterious villains who, once exposed by Batman's detective work, led him on a wild rooftop chase. And it ended when Batman, descending like a Fury on a long thin rope from an upper ledge of a multilevel building, swept the three villains skulking on a lower ledge straight to their deaths in the street below. Edward read through the story hurriedly this time, again struck by how untypical it was of Batman to kill anyone with such calculated and brutal precision. Well, these comic books seemed to be getting worse and worse lately. It might be time to try to wean Jack onto other less violent reading matter.

"Did you think that was the right thing for Batman to do?" he said to Jack after finishing the sequence.

"He could hardly have had much of a choice," Jack replied, choosing words that seemed syntactically too sophisticated for the boy to have uttered. Edward looked up from the comic to search the boy's face and realized that he'd gotten things mixed up.

It wasn't Jack at all, sitting beside him. It was Jean-Marc. And it was he who had uttered those words, speaking not to Edouard but to the three Sherpas who stood gazing down at them. It was almost dark, and the double nylon tents had already been set up on a wide rocky plateau that formed an outcropping of the trail they had been following.

The Sherpas were staring at him in a way that struck him as both awkward and uncomfortable. "What is it? What happened?" Edouard said, bewildered. "How did we get here?"

"You don't know?" Jean-Marc said, turning back to him.

"Know what?"

"*Mon dieu,* is it possible you really were—sleepwalking?" He gazed at the Sherpas again and said something in Mandarin, to which they responded slowly and—it seemed to Edouard, intently aware of their expressions—somewhat sadly.

"They are saying, it doesn't matter how it happened. The fact is, you killed three men. They're Buddhists, remember. It offends them deeply when—"

"What are you talking about? I *killed* somebody? When? How? What happened?" He struggled to his feet.

As Jean-Marc continued to stare at him, Edouard added, "Wait! Sleepwalking? A dream? But it was in that comic book. A real dream. Where Batman killed three hoodlums. He came down at them from an overhanging roof on a rope and swept them off." He broke off suddenly. "Are you saying it was more than that? What the hell did happen? Will you please explain it to me?"

Jean-Marc peered into Edouard's face. "You really don't know?" He pressed his gloved hands to his cheeks, half hidden within his fur hood. "Then you really were sleepwalking. There's no other explanation. And even then—" He turned unexpectedly to the Sherpas and issued a brief order. The younger Sherpa moved toward the end of the ledge where it was terraced above a smaller ledge some ten meters down, clearly visible in the still-glowing embers of a dying campfire. There were guns and bits of camping gear strewn about on that lower terrace. But no campers. Now, the Sherpa retrieved the end of the climb-line, which had been dangling down close to the dying fire. He returned, recoiling the loose end, following the line's sinuous trail to where its other end was still wrapped about a high pointed rock at the very spot where Edouard sat. Jean-Marc took it and showed it to Edouard.

"You don't remember using this? Our climb-line?" Here, he plucked up a segment somewhere in the middle of the coil and pointed to where parts of the rope had splayed in broken bits around its own center. "Or how this part got frayed on the rocks as you swung down on it? You don't remember?" And as Edouard stared in dumbfounded silence, the other added, "No, of course you don't. Because in your right mind, you couldn't have done it in a dozen years of training. Not you. I could have perhaps. But not so smoothly. When the soldiers reached the lower ledge and set up camp, we had you resting out here, with your oxygen on, because you were slow in coming out of the hypoxia. We didn't even make a fire just to be sure we weren't detected. But the air was still, so Ardong and I sat out here with you, outside the tent, watching you. And then, a dislodged pebble, a scraping sound. The soldiers had flashlamps; they saw us and started shooting. And you, you suddenly unstrapped the oxygen and grabbed the rope, tying it to this rock here, and then, as though you'd been doing it all your life, you swooped down on them and caught all three of them with your feet and swept them off the ledge. And when the Sherpas say a demon possessed you, I'm inclined to agree with them, even though I never before even considered the possibility that demons exist."

Chapter Sixteen

was the only one who knew. I, Alvin. Not Edouard Bazenrüd and
not Edward Horgan. The Sherpa, Lobsang Tsienpu, a sophisticated
Buddhist, may have had an inkling. And, of course, in the *gompa,*
the monastery they would finally reach after getting well to the east
of Lhasa, the *khempo* would understand. But that was yet to come.
For the moment, it was Kay who was calling for explanations.

We had moved to the screened porch that looked out on the
Banana River, hazy with the late afternoon sun so that we could
barely see Merritt Island on the opposite shore.

"I've been able to swallow a lot of things since you got tangled
up with Thongden, things like consciousness visiting and having you
meet up with my imaginary childhood companion," Kay said. "And
even time shifts, so that what should have happened yesterday is happening only now, while tomorrow somehow gets set back to yesterday. But this? You killed someone during a dream about Batman? Up
until now, it was all twisted and crazy and revealing but never deadly.
Three men dead. It's turning into some kind of scary witchcraft."

I acknowledged that the whole experiment had taken on a grim
aspect. But there were much higher stakes in this game than the one
Thongden led me through with Superman. And the deaths were

inadvertent. Because we were dealing with a very volatile and capricious force that represented itself as Batman. "And what's more," I added, "it was completely innocent on Horgan's part. He thought he was reading a Batman story to his son. And he didn't even approve of the violence in the story."

"And you say you understand how it happened?"

"I understand that there was a bleedthrough so that I had managed to bring my consciousness into Bazenrüd's. But he had no consciousness of *me*. Almost like one of those cases of multiple personalities you sometimes hear about. But in this instance, I was the visitor to Bazenrüd's consciousness. And not just a passive visitor either. Until now, I always thought that you could visit another consciousness without affecting it. But this time, I apparently brought all that Bruce Wayne baggage with me.

"Of course, it had to be Thongden's doing. His purpose was to clear up my ambivalent attitude to finance by putting me into the shoes of a financial wizard like Bazenrüd. The trouble is, I had other baggage of my own, all those years of doing Batman, so that in a sense I'd caught some of the pent-up rage of Bruce Wayne. Or, more accurately, Wayne's pent-up rage provided a fitting analogue of some deeper rage in me, something still to be worked out. But after that sleepwalking episode, it's obvious that there can be a positive side to such a rage."

"How can you call killing those soldiers something positive?"

"It saved our lives. Only a dyed-in-the-wool Buddhist wouldn't see that. At least, that's how I felt about it during those moments when I became aware of my presence in Bazenrüd. And remember, it wasn't deliberate. It really was a kind of sleepwalking. Did you know that sleepwalkers can drive cars through heavy traffic with great skill and then not remember a thing about it when they wake up? In fact, we all seem to have so many different consciousnesses operating in us at the same time, I wonder how . . ."

"Wonder how, what?"

I shrugged. "Wonder how we can ever get back to our basic selves,
I guess. How do we ever learn the difference? You've heard the old
Chinese question, Am I a butterfly dreaming I'm a man, or a man
dreaming I'm a butterfly? But, I'm getting ahead of myself again. I
learned a lot more about it when we got to the *gompa,* the monastery
that was to be our last stop before I set out for Minya Konka, on my
own. Or rather, on Bazenrüd's own."

After the encounter with the soldiers, there was a profound change
in the mood of the party. Though the Sherpas continued to provide
the guidance they'd signed on for, there was less socializing with their
clients. They maintained, at best, a cautious acceptance. There was
a long way yet to travel and many dangers on the way, both natural
and human. But after a couple of weeks of alternately trekking overland and then using their inflatable boats to move downriver, they
managed to get safely east of Lhasa.

Two days later, without incident, they reached the place where
the Huang Po took a bend for the south. It was now time to leave the
river and continue due west on foot to complete the last part of their
journey to the monastery.

They had been two days into this final trek when Ardong, who
had been reconnoitering some two hundred yards ahead of the others, suddenly signaled with an upflung arm. They hurried to join
him. He pointed to a spot several yards to the left of where they were
standing. The trail here was broad, consisting of loose snow over
hard packed ice that glittered blindingly in the sunlight. But Lobsang
quickly took in the cause of Ardong's concern: a long area where
the glitter broke into short regular segments. In English, Lobsang
explained to Jean-Marc and Edouard, "Look carefully and you will
see the tracks of an armored troop carrier. Somewhere along here,
we were passed by a military unit going in the same direction. It is

most fortunate that they did not see us. But they were traveling along the left edge of the trail, which dips below us at the point where they must have passed. In any case, I do not think they were looking for us, or for anyone."

"What do you mean?" Jean-Marc queried. "What was their purpose out here, then?"

Lobsang responded with a grave movement of the head. "Why would they send a military unit with an armored car? Not for any small parties of stragglers like ourselves. No, this would have been a larger operation. They must have been looking for the monastery. Why else would they be out this way? There is nothing else out here. I had heard already that the Han Chinese are destroying all monasteries. Now they are seemingly determined to finish this one." As he spoke, he moved some yards to the left so that he could examine the tracks more closely. The others followed watchfully after him. Then Lobsang paused, bent lower as he examined an outline in the snow. "Another set of footprints. But there is something strange about them."

"How do you mean, strange?" Edouard said.

"What I see is not normal walking. As though someone had passed the soldiers and managed to go on ahead. You see, the prints are so far apart, it is obviously a trance walker. Someone who must have gone on to warn the monastery. A *lon-gompa* can easily slip past the soldiers and get there well ahead of them."

"Will the monks resist? Can they?" Jean-Marc asked.

"They will not fight and they will not resist. It may be we will arrive and find everything destroyed. Our journey wasted."

"It is perhaps not worth it for us to go on," Ardong suggested in Tibetan.

"But we will continue, nevertheless," Lobsang said. "Because," he added, "there is always some possibility we may not foresee. Certainly not if we turn back now."

Returning to the trail, the little group continued on for the rest of that day. Conversation among them had almost completely died down. They moved with leaden steps even though the trail at this juncture already brought the distant peak into view within whose glacial purlieus, according to Lobsang, the monastery was located. The conviction was strong that they would arrive only to discover the worst. Even Edouard, who had all along been buoyed up by his own private sense of mission, was beginning to feel that their long and arduous journey would now turn out to have been futile. But just before their trek brought them to the moment when it was time to start seeking a campsite for the night, Ardong, who had the vision of an eagle, spotted some tiny black dots far ahead. "Soldiers," he warned. "They are coming back."

This was enough to send the whole party into a flurry of activity. There was no place along that open segment of the trail that could hide them, no cave, no rocks, no crevices in the snow. They broke into a fury of digging at the trail's farthest edge, using small axes and shovels to scoop shallow places from the frozen path, enough for each of them to crawl into and lie flat. Only Ardong did not follow this procedure. His job was to sweep the gouged-out particles of ice and snow over his companions, effectively hiding them from the casual glances of the approaching military unit. Then, taking a large white canvas that was part of one of their tents, Ardong fell on the ground and drew it over him so that he appeared to be no more than an anomalous blob of ice at the point where the trail backed against a small hillock on the side farthest from the soldiers. Then they waited.

Within moments, three half-tracks, with soldiers clinging to them, churned past, moving at a speed that indicated they were clearly hastening back and looking for no one. Minutes later, the Sherpas and their two Caucasian companions abandoned their hiding places and eyed each other uncertainly. The convoy of soldiers was already out of sight.

"They did not seem to have any prisoners," Ardong suggested tentatively.

"From which you conclude, what?" asked the second Sherpa.

"Almost always they take prisoners to bring back for public humiliation," Lobsang explained to Jean-Marc and Bazenrüd.

"They were moving as if they had other things to do than bother taking prisoners," said the second Sherpa.

"You're saying they must have killed them all?"

Lobsang refused to surrender to pessimism. "Again, there are always unforeseen possibilities."

"You keep saying that as if you know something we don't," Edouard said.

"Only that an observant person cannot have lasted as many years as I without noting that too often the unforeseen takes the place of the anticipated. So I no longer anticipate. We will camp here for tonight. And tomorrow, we will go on to the monastery."

It was a dispirited group that broke camp the next morning and took up their trek to the monastery. Jean-Marc and the two younger Sherpas were glumly silent. Edouard was grim. Only Lobsang seemed to be his usual self, unhindered by any thoughts less purposive than reaching Dango Gompa. By now, it also seemed that yesterday afternoon's near encounter with the soldiers had eclipsed the disapproving mood created by Edouard's earlier somnambulistic killing of the soldiers on the ledge. Fortunately, the weather held up, providing a windless day that allowed them to keep their hoods open. They had only the glare of sun on ice to contend with, and for this they wore heavy tinted goggles. It was early afternoon when they reached the shadows of the peak toward which they had been moving all day. They could now remove the goggles. Lobsang pointed toward a promontory about a mile ahead where the path seemed to penetrate directly into the great peak. "It is through there, but," he broke off, sounding puzzled.

"What is it?" said Jean-Marc.

"The path, it does not seem to continue. But perhaps we are too far off yet." He waved his hand, signaling the others to follow, and started forward. It took them twenty minutes to reach the point where the path came to an abrupt end. Lobsang's doubts were confirmed. In front of them was a sheer wall of ice.

"It is not possible," the old Sherpa said. "I have been here before. At this point, there should be a passage that leads directly to Dango Gompa."

"Look," said Ardong, examining the far side of the trail. "The footprints of the soldiers, they go off in this direction. If we follow—"

He did not have to finish. In a moment, the others swarmed across the path, following the trail of the soldiers. But after some half hour of walking, the tracks ended and reversed.

"Could they somehow have found the monastery and destroyed it?" Edouard said to Jean-Marc.

"There are no such signs. The soldiers apparently were as confused as we are. Look at the footprints. They finally stop here and head back. Perhaps we were all misinformed. The monastery is simply not in this place."

"I could not be mistaken," Lobsang insisted. "Once I have walked a trail, I never forget it. Let us return to where the entrance should be, back where the path ends. I have something in mind."

In a few moments they were once more facing the solid wall of ice that blocked the path. "I keep remembering," Lobsang explained, "the footprints of the *lon-gompa* who went ahead of the soldiers. Clearly, the monks were warned of the danger."

"But what could they have done? This wall of ice could not have been created by the monks. Even a team of engineers—"

"But there was something they could do," Lobsang said. He moved closer to the wall and rapped on it with his gloved hand. "It is solid indeed. Solid as the mountain itself." He turned to the others, his back to the wall now. "Please, everyone step back and settle down. We will bivouac here for a short while. There is something I must try, but I must not be interrupted. Seat yourselves. And please maintain silence." He spoke in English, then repeated himself to the other Sherpas in their own tongue. They looked at one another in bewilderment, but without further questioning, they began to settle themselves, laying down coverings from their packs to allow them to squat on the ground. Lobsang turned his back on them and assumed the lotus position. In moments, facing the great shield of ice, he had entered into deep meditation.

The day gradually changed from a light-drenched warming blaze multiplied in the mirror surfaces of the enormous vertical glacial wall until, the sun having drifted from sight as it crossed to the peak's other side, the landscape looked cold and gray. The men were becoming chilled and restless, and Edouard, in his growing impatience, was about to call a halt to what he presumed was a needless and ineffectual ritual on Lobsang's part. Somehow, the grayness prevented his seeing the change. Only Ardong, ever alert, noticed it but said nothing until Lobsang, getting to his feet, called everyone's attention to it. He pointed straight ahead to where the wall of ice had blocked their path.

"Look."

And everyone looked. Their astonishment was expressed in a prolonged silence. The wonder that lay before them was a long thin opening in the glacial wall, a natural way of ingress that marked the continuation of the path they had been following.

"*Merde!*" Jean-Marc exclaimed. "I don't believe this. He dissolved the glacier."

But Edouard, in a flash of insight, suddenly understood. "No," he said. "There was nothing there to begin with. Except an illusion. And Lobsang's concentration put an end to it. Am I right?" he finished by addressing himself to the older Sherpa.

Lobsang nodded. "It was a thought form. I knew it had to be.

One of those things that adepts can shape into solid matter, sometimes even living matter. You have heard of human personalities, *tulpas,* created by deep meditation? We have long been familiar with the fact that mindfulness can create form, both human and natural. This natural barrier was obviously created to hide the monastery from the soldiers after they received a warning from the *lon-gompa.* But," he added, shaking his head, "they must indeed have a very powerful *rimpoche* to have created such a barrier in so short a time. As it turned out, it was not very stable anyway, or I could not have had the mental force to dissolve it."

"Then the monastery must be just beyond the opening."

"About three kilometers, as I remember," Lobsang said.

The others were already gathering up their gear when he added, "We should be there within the hour."

They could see it from where they stood, just beyond the entrance to the pass. There was a cluster of small white structures consisting of a *lhabrang,* a monks' dormitory, and numerous separate monks' dwellings around the much larger central building of the temple. For some moments, Edouard and his party gazed at the sight of the monastery limned against the hillside by the slanting rays of the setting sun. Then abruptly, everything vanished. A sudden snow squall had dropped a heavy curtain across their line of sight. In seconds, the thickly falling flakes had engulfed the little group of travelers. Edouard could scarcely make out Jean-Marc's looming shape as he stood beside him on the trail. The voices of the three Sherpas who had gone ahead several yards sent back muffled warnings. Edouard could barely distinguish Lobsang's words.

"Try to go forward. Try to keep to the trail. It is not safe to stand here. We must seek shelter before the drifts grow too high." There followed further admonitions to Edouard and Jean-Marc to grope their way forward and join hands with their guides, who knew by long experience how to keep to the now invisible trail.

And then, Jean-Marc no longer seemed to be standing beside him. Edouard moved forward cautiously, calling out the other's name. Almost immediately, he heard Jean-Marc's reply, but could not make out from which direction he was calling. The swirling snow formed thick vortices that channeled the sound in shifting and indeterminate ways. At first, it seemed as though his friend was waiting directly ahead of him. Then he seemed to hear a voice far over to the left. And as he veered in that direction, he knew from his unstable footing that he had somehow reached the outermost edge of the trail. Reaching out, he could feel a pile of heavy rocks or ice slabs of the sort that had all along marked the boundaries of the trail. Veering back, and moving forward again, he encountered similar rocky formations to his right but too soon for him to have crossed the width of the trail. He knew that he had inadvertently reversed direction. In a reaction of near panic, he reversed himself once more and tried calling out, but the sheer opacity of the massed flakes only threw his voice back at him.

By now, the depth of the gathering drifts was making walking difficult in any direction. Instead of fighting, he let himself sink into a moment of calm. And then he heard it: a deep, heavy sound that seemed to rise up out of the ground itself. It was as though several gigantic tubas were plunging their low melancholy frequencies deep down into the earth and out again. As he continued to listen, he could also distinguish deep-throated, bassoonlike sounds accompanied by the rhythm of bass drums, all of which were now sending their sonorous vibrations despite the viscous roiling sheets of snow. Whether purposively or not, the monastery was radiating a signal through the ground over which there now seemed to come higher-pitched, more directional sounds whose point of origin he could pinpoint.

Moving slowly and carefully as the drifts grew around him, Edouard traced his way toward those guiding high notes. Thrusting through the rapidly building drifts, he found himself tiring quickly.

The high altitude took its toll of strenuous effort. He slowed, despite himself, but struggled on for what seemed a long time, until he began to recognize in himself the dangerous impulse to cease striving and lie down in the snow. But at the same time, the horns became more urgent in their summons, encouraging him to continue on. After what seemed endless unimaginable effort, his hand came up against the stone lintel of a building. He found the door and pounded heavily on it, using the hard surface of the tea bowl he had grown accustomed to carrying inside his parka. The sounds reverberated dully. The door opened and Edouard fell exhausted as strong hands grasped him and dragged him inside.

He fell asleep, but only, it seemed, for seconds. When he opened his eyes, he was sitting up, his back against a wall, his hood removed, as an elderly monk bent over him. A few other monks had joined Jean-Marc and the Sherpas who stood in a semicircle watching him. Along the opposite wall, Edouard observed guttering rows of smoky butter lamps. There were numerous monks sitting about, lying on mats, and otherwise making their home within what was clearly a *lhabrang,* a dormitory. He drank slowly from the bowl of hot buttered tea that the elderly monk now held out to him. At the same time, the old man was saying something to him in Tibetan.

Lobsang stepped forward and translated. "He is saying that it is very rare for a *piling* to appear in this monastery. You must be the one the Great Lama is expecting."

Edouard shook his head. "Not I, surely. No one could be expecting me here."

Again Lobsang translated. The elderly monk pressed his palms together. He seemed to be introducing himself. His name sounded to Edouard something like Delwha. Again he spoke and Lobsang translated.

"It is not possible that you should come here and not be expected."

Edouard frowned and looked toward Lobsang. "Are you sure you got that right?"

Lobsang smiled. "It is you who must get it right," he assured Edouard. "Your Western mind sees things in a cause-and-effect sequence. Here, they see events as connected like the spokes of a wheel. You cannot separate your coming here from their expecting you."

Slowly, Edouard got to his feet. He was feeling a little weak but otherwise clearheaded and in command of himself. Looking from the old monk to Lobsang, he said, "But were they really expecting us?"

Lobsang smiled again. "We are here. Therefore they have been expecting us." He turned to Delwha and translated this last bit of colloquy. Delwha shook his head vigorously and spoke quickly in Tibetan to Lobsang.

It was now Lobsang who frowned as he turned to explain to Edouard. "He says I am essentially correct. We were expected. But there is more. The Great Lama had, in fact, already announced our coming before he went into his deep meditation."

"When was that?" Edouard asked.

Lobsang posed the question to Delwha. The old monk replied with an upraised finger and a single word.

Now Lobsang looked truly puzzled as he turned to Edouard. "A year ago," he said.

Delwha added more, and Lobsang translated. "The Great Lama was sealed in his meditation chamber a year ago to this very day. Even as we arrived, Delwha tells me, the seal on the Lama's meditation chamber was being broken and he was emerging from his long retreat."

"Now I really do not understand," Edouard confessed.

"I am also at a loss," Lobsang agreed. He turned to Delwha and there was a further exchange. Then Delwha bowed and started away.

"He says," Lobsang began, "that he is not the one to explain these matters to us. But he will now go and announce our arrival to Khempo Khadup."

Somewhat puzzled, Edouard sat down on some pillows alongside Jean-Marc, who nodded at him in silent acknowledgment that he, too, was puzzled. Occasionally, the other monks eyed them curiously but did not approach, although they could be seen whispering among themselves and sometimes pointing toward the small group of visitors. About a half hour later, a servant approached the group from the far end of the *lhabrang*. He bowed before Edouard, indicating that his message was for him alone.

"I am to conduct you to the *khempo*'s quarters, Kushab."

Edouard got to his feet, looked searchingly at his companions, each of whom signaled a negative to his unspoken question as to whether they should accompany him. Shrugging, he trailed after the servant by himself, following the man to the far end of the *lhabrang,* through a small curtained passageway, into a small but well-appointed apartment. Just ahead of him was the *khempo,* the abbot, seated on a raised, straight-backed chair, wearing ordinary monk's clothing to which was added a brocade vest and a yellow hat. But to Edouard's great surprise, he found himself looking into the smiling eyes of a boy of hardly more than fourteen. Even so, the maturity of this very young person's demeanor made him realize that he might be confronting one of those unique Tibetan personalities known as a *tulku,* something he had heard about several times during the course of the long journey with the Sherpas. So he understood that a *tulku* was supposed to be a reincarnated Lama, in full possession of the wisdom acquired in an earlier life. At the time, he had accepted the information as part of the mythos of the Tibetan culture. But he was not prepared to find himself in the presence of a living, breathing *tulku.*

Indeed, for some moments, he believed that this meeting was

somehow being staged for his benefit, although he could not begin to imagine why. He would have liked to question the young man who sat before him with such assurance, but without access to the Tibetan language, the best he could offer was a tentative bow.

"Put aside your doubts, Kushab Bazenrüd. I am indeed what you suspect me to be."

Eduoard stared. The words, spoken in English, echoed clearly in his head. But the *khempo*'s lips had not moved. Had he really spoken?

"I have indeed," the *khempo* seemed to reply, again without moving his lips. "But the method does not rely on the physical body since it involves direct thought exchange."

"You mean," Edouard responded, "telepathy." He spoke aloud.

"I did not use that term for a reason. Telepathy implies a sending of signals between entities separated by space. Here, there is no sending and receiving. Here, we are joined in a unity of mind. Remember, there is not really 'your mind' and 'my mind'. There is only mind, which we all share."

"But it's all under your control. I don't really have any connection with it."

The *khempo* slid somewhat awkwardly off his high seat and stood before Edouard, shorter than the latter by a third of a meter. He was indeed a small boy, especially for a Tibetan, a people whose high-altitude existence seemed somehow to breed a taller race. "You will have your connection, at the right time."

"I don't understand."

"Come with me. I will show you."

He led the way from his quarters into another adjoining room, this one a large, well-lit chamber with openings along the northern wall that brought the brightness of daylight inside. In lieu of glass, those same openings were glazed with a type of translucent, oiled membrane that helped retain the heat given off by several burning braziers of yak dung while providing a maximum of natural light. All of which seemed to be for the benefit of a tall, hatless, shaven-headed monk who sat hunched over a large table on which a frame of cloth, hardened by a surface of dried glue, lay white and empty before him. The man held a brush in his hand, and he now dipped this into one of several pots of coloring that sat on the table alongside the frame. The monk did not look up as Edouard and the *khempo* drew alongside. He seemed not to notice them at all, so concentrated was he on the blank canvas before him. Holding the brush with its glob of color, he sat for a long moment in rapt contemplation of the canvas.

"You will note, Kushab," the youthful *khempo* appeared to be saying, "that this daring monk seems lost in his study of the empty space he plans to decorate. And, in a sense, he is truly lost, because in the emptiness before him, he knows that all possible expressions of the graphic medium are being offered him. Would not an ordinary man be overwhelmed at selecting a single statement from such a totality?"

"What is your point, exactly, Khempo?" Edouard asked, still speaking aloud.

"Just that at this moment, for this monk, potential is all. But there is no life."

The *khempo* reached up and took the arm of his puzzled guest, and drew him away from the table. "Come, let us go for a walk."

He led Edouard silently through various chambers and cells of the monastery, allowing him to observe the multitude of artifacts in cloth and color that decorated the central temple as well as the smaller monks' quarters and even the kitchens. There was no further attempt by the *khempo* to resume what he called "direct thought exchange." He seemed to be carefully letting Edouard form his own impressions.

The effect on Edouard was peculiarly cleansing. At first, as he trod silently alongside the diminutive *khempo,* with his youthful appearance contrasting so oddly with his mature and rather introspective demeanor, he began to experience a rush of images that expressed, not so much new ways of seeing, or thinking or feeling, but rather called into question what he already tended to draw from sensory experience. The walk was a kind of gentle assault on his Western way of seeing things. It was as though the *khempo* had chosen this quiet way of preparing Edouard for some more embracing thought yet to be revealed. For at last, they returned to the cell where the monk still sat before his canvas.

Only now, the canvas was no longer empty. There was a jagged line of warm color that leaped from the upper left quadrant, crossed near the center, and stopped abruptly at the upper edge of the lower right quadrant. A simple enough change, but the canvas had taken on a kind of tension. The blankness had become expectation.

Now the *khempo* was initiating direct thought exchange once more. "Note what has happened, Kushab. A line has been placed on the canvas, and suddenly the possibilities are limited. Defined by the line and its unique characteristics. And each stroke the monk makes limits him even more. It would appear, then, that every action is a step away from the infinite. That is the common wisdom, and it is not correct."

"And why not?" Edouard asked.

"To begin with, the blank canvas was in total balance. It rested in infinite equilibrium. It was simply nothing about nothing. But when a line sets up a disequilibrium, then there is the beginning of life. The painter, of course, strives to bring the equilibrium back and adds other strokes of the brush, setting up, alas, further disequilibriums. More strokes and the painting becomes more complex. When does it stop? What is the painter aiming at, a renewal of equilibrium? No, no, that is the danger, that a single stroke might so connect all the others that once again the painting returns to equilibrium. And it will be a failure. It will die.

"But there is a third way. The way we call the incremental way. By proceeding carefully, the opposing forces do reach a kind of balance. They continue to pull on each other, but neither force triumphs. Always, there are small imbalances, but they tend to adjust themselves into a finer balance, which is then pulled into a new imbalance. These are, you might say, the joys of life, the dance of being momentarily off balance and momentarily in balance. This is also what truth is like. It resembles the uniqueness of the created thing, its perpetually changing, living face. In this will you surely find the infinite, of which the infinity of the blank canvas is but the unrealized possibility."

"In effect," Edouard said in a flash of vision, "you are describing a kind of vibration."

"Yes. A motion in opposing directions which, as it waxes and wanes, creates the music of the dance. Does that appeal to you?"

Edouard was thoughtful for a moment. "Is it possible for someone who understands this vibratory process very well—"

"Do not hesitate. Your thoughts follow an important track."

"—can such a one, by affecting the vibration, change the music of the dance?"

The *khempo*'s dark, bright youthful eyes fixed on Edouard for what seemed a long time. "That is the reason you have come here, is it not?"

"You read my mind," Edouard acknowledged. "But I would not have been able to express it so clearly had you not just demonstrated the shifting equilibrium of the dance. Suddenly I realized that what you revealed clarifies the very danger I have come here to prevent."

"Because," Khempo explained, "you have taken on a mission not entirely your own."

Edouard, who had already had intimations of such a possibility in a number of recent anomalous experiences, looked quietly at the *khempo,* anticipating that at last, he was about to be offered some kind of explanation.

"Lobsang told me about your attack on the Han Chinese soldiers on the way here."

"And you can explain it for me?"

"You must first ask yourself who you are."

Edouard lifted his hands in a gesture of diffidence. "In your terms or mine?"

"When you say 'mine', you are thinking, of course, of Edouard Bazenrüd. And you are raising the question of whether we Buddhists accept the reality of the self to begin with. Leaving all that aside, let us look more closely at this Bazenrüd self of yours. The one that came here with a mission. Can you tell me about that?"

"There's a difficulty explaining the Bazenrüd self too. It is, uh, a purely cultivated identity."

"That is an odd way of putting it. But to my understanding, all identities are, as you say, cultivated."

"More precisely, I'm not really Bazenrüd. I'm a man named Edward Horgan, who has simply put on this Bazenrüd identity like a suit of clothes. It's also part of my being here. Part of my involvement in this mission, if you like." He broke out of his now wordless speech with a broad gesture, extending his arms as though embracing the entire monastery. "And there's more. While I'm certain that I am Edward Horgan, there seems also to be someone else. I don't know how to explain this. But there was another personality behind that attack on the Han Chinese soldiers. Someone I really don't know. Someone I haven't a shred of knowledge about. But he seems to have some important connection with me."

"That would be Batman?" the *khempo* suggested.

"No. Someone called Alvin."

Chapter Seventeen

"The Buddhists were wrong, Kay," I said.

She had been curled up on the couch listening so intently that she was beginning to get a little stiff. Now, she stretched out her legs, sat up, and settled her feet on the floor. At the same time she extended her arms in a fierce effort to unlock a gathering physical torpor. But even while taking care of these physical needs, her attention was still fully focused on me.

"If the Buddha really believed life was suffering," I continued, "why didn't he himself escape it? He actually chose suffering. He chose to come back and rescue those who were victims of meaningless suffering. How can there be a meaning without a striving? And how can there be true striving without pain? And what strives? Who is the striver? It is the self. Can the self then be an illusion? Can an illusion be concerned with meaning?"

Kay brushed aside my philosophical meandering. "How did he know about Alvin?"

"The Buddha?"

"No, silly. Bazenrüd."

I took a few steps toward the window, peered out briefly, then turned back to her. "I think once I became aware of the bleedthrough,

I felt it ought to be apparent from his end as well. And maybe I had some help."

"What help?"

"I don't imagine Thongden was just passively waiting for me to come back and report to him. I think he worked to increase everyone's awareness. And why wouldn't he? He had a lot at stake in this whole affair."

"But how could he do anything?"

"I didn't really know at first. Except I knew he had to. Or it would have been the end to things."

"The end to things," Kay repeated. "What does that mean?"

"I can tell you now," I said. "From my present perspective, nothing could be clearer. But back then, there was Alvin-awareness and Edouard-awareness. And then—"

I turned to her suddenly. I knew my expression must have been somber by the way she drew back. "Then—what?" she asked in a voice that sounded almost as if she didn't want to hear it. I really must have looked strange.

"I simply stopped being. I was gone. Nonexistent."

"You mean, dead?"

I shook my head. "It's very hard to explain. When you're dead, you're still you, even though, well, you're out of it. I'm not sure I can explain how this was different. There just wasn't any Edouard Bazenrüd or Edward Horgan or Alvin. But I was still there. Not I. I didn't mean that. Just awareness. Pure awareness. There was no sense of I at all."

"Oh no, wait. You were still there, how? Like a puff of smoke or something?"

"No, no, listen. When you're dead, as I said, you're out of it. But I wasn't out of it. The part that was *me* was gone, but an awareness was there, a consciousness. Something was conscious but it wasn't me. It was just consciousness. You remember that whole Buddhist idea about the personality not being real, that it's just an accidental collection of sensations. Much closer to that puff of smoke you just mentioned. Well, I discovered that when you take that away, that I-ness, there's not *nothing*. Which explains why the Buddha came back. Why there was something to come back for. Because of that not-nothing. And not something either. It's like," I did a half-turn about the room and then I pointed toward a place just ahead of me where the wall met the ceiling. "It's like being that mountain."

"What mountain?"

"Sorry. The one I was trying to climb as I left the monastery for Minya Konka. Suddenly, there it was. Instead of me, the climber confronting that mountain, I was the mountain. All that need for climbing was gone. The need for anything, for achieving anything, getting to Minya Konka, gone. Because I was already there. Everything accomplished. Everything complete. What filled my awareness was that I had been living everything backwards, trapped in a kind of arrow of one-way time. With everything broken into little bits and pieces and all my life I had been struggling to line the pieces up again, and then—" I made a gesture of helplessness.

"You had a revelation," Kay proposed. "One of those mystical unifying—"

"No, nothing so grandiose. There was just the realization that I had always known, that I was part of the knowing. Nothing more complicated than, well, a sneeze. Or stepping over a crack in the sidewalk."

That was when I noticed the impish smile steal over Kay's face. "In that case," she said. "Why didn't you come right home? Why did you have to stay away so long?"

I responded in kind. "I had to wait for the train to stop before I could get off. You can't just jump off any time you feel like it."

"Of course not."

"And even though I knew, I had to go through the whole thing just the same. But because I knew, it was different. It was easier. And, yes, I knew about my Alvin side. Or rather, I knew about the different shared identities involved in this mission. If I hadn't known, it wouldn't have been possible for me, or rather, for Edouard, to learn *lon-gompa*. Not in so short a time. Usually it takes twenty years."

"You mean trance-walking?"

"Yes, exactly."

"And why didn't you need twenty years like everyone else?"

"Because just lining up all the bits and pieces of life as presented through the one-way arrow of time, just doing that, and getting rid of them, that usually takes at least ninety-nine percent of the learning. And I had already arrived there. I already knew that there was no outside world as we normally understand it. We're all inculcated with this belief that out there is an independently existing and stubborn world that we can figure out and try to manipulate. All our science is based on that. But when I discovered that I could exist and not be anyone at all, then I knew the world out there wasn't anything specific either. So that when I had to travel through all that terrible mountainous terrain to get to Minya Konka, all I had to do was shrink it down to manageable size. In other words, I could change the so-called outside reality. I could shrink it down in such a way that I could walk across it as though it were a scale model. And one step would carry me a hundred yards instead of a couple of feet. You see? By changing the outside image, I made it manageable. That's what I had to practice: reducing the size I already had in mind. Concentrating on shrinking it down."

As I explained this, Kay sat up, stiffly attentive. "Now wait. You're telling me that by thought, you can change anything you don't like in your surroundings? Like you could turn this condo into a twenty-room mansion?"

"Maybe I could," I confessed, smiling at her. "But I'd have to concentrate on it for about ten years. And keep concentrating. I wouldn't have time for much else. No, it doesn't work like that. On the other hand, learning to concentrate on where I put my feet, that doesn't take much. But even that, they warned me, wouldn't hold up too well. If I wanted to put in an extra year of training, maybe I could get back. All they trained me for was just enough to get to Minya Konka. Nobody ever figured I'd be able to make it back that way."

"You mean, you took a chance on never being able to come back?"

"Remember, it wasn't my decision. It was Edouard's. He knew he had to do it, no matter what it cost."

"And you had nothing to say about it?"

"We were aware of each other, but it was his stage."

"I don't understand that," Kay said with a kind of angry finality, as though expressing her disapproval of Edouard's having dragged me through such danger.

"I don't either, exactly." I flashed a smile at her. "Maybe in another twenty years."

She got off the couch and threw her arms around my neck and hugged me. "I don't want to hear anymore right now," she said. "I just want to feel grateful for a while."

"About what?"

"That you got back, somehow."

What I told Kay was the truth. But simplified. I left out all the details of how the young *khempo* took Edouard, took him by the hand in fact, as though Edouard were the child, and he, the child-ruler of the *gompa*, the adult.

"You must start your training at once. There is little time. It is all part of Ugen Rimpoche's plan, his reason for awakening on this very day."

"I see. But, where are you taking me?"

"To the *tasha*, the chamber where Rimpoche waits for you."

"He wishes to see me?" Edouard said, impressed by what he understood as a special honor.

"He will teach you. You will become his *chela,* his disciple."

"Just like that? With no preparation? Does he communicate the same way you do?"

"He communicates in real speech. Rimpoche knows 378 different languages."

They were passing through a long, low-ceilinged corridor with whitewashed walls and none of that decoration so common to every bit of architectural surface Edouard had observed since coming here. Before he could even raise the question, the *khempo* was answering it. "The emptiness of the walls and ceilings are the first stages of the emptying of all former presuppositions as you enter the presence of Ugen Rimpoche." And then he glanced quizzically at Edouard. "But you were going to ask me something else, and I lost it."

"About these languages Rimpoche has learned. Has he lived outside of Tibet?"

"In your sense, no. But in the real sense, you can say that he lives outside the limits of any particular place. His mind, to use a Western term, is nonlocal."

"But how—"

"Nonlocality is not an easy concept to grasp. If you need to see things and be anywhere, you must be where those things are. The prejudice of simple location, as one of your great English philosophers explained."

"Who was that?"

"A man called Alfred. Alfred North Whitehead."

Edouard shook his head. "I haven't read him. But I've heard of him. But you, you have read him?"

"No," the young *khempo* explained. "I learned of Alfred from Ugen Rimpoche."

There was no further discussion. They had reached the end of the corridor. Ahead was a narrow opening without a door. They moved in single file, the *khempo* leading as each stooped, then stepped abruptly into the *tasha*.

It was not the smooth-faced old man seated on a pile of cushions in the center of the cell that first caught Edouard's attention. It was the unexpected and pervasive warmth, even though there was no sign of the usual altar with its constant small fire of yak dung. Not even a butter lamp flickered to send its meager calidity into the room. Through a single large window, the waning liquid sunlight coated the bare walls in a chrome yellow splendor. But that wasn't the source of the warmth either. It was from Ugen Rimpoche himself, squatting on his mound of pillows and dressed in thin, brightly colored garments woven from the finer hairs of the yak instead of the usual coarser skins the rest of the monks used. But Edouard needed an extra moment to realize that this tiny old man was indeed emanating heat.

A trickle of laughter, almost a giggle, shook the old man as his face creased with an odd, almost boyish delight. "You never been around human radiator before, Mr. Edward Horgan Bazenrüd, or however you call yourself." The voice was thin, almost piping, but clear. The English was marked by a strange and somewhat careless use of verb forms and indefinite articles. "It was the long meditation, you see? You accumulate extra heat. I'll be like this whole month. Then have to look to outside sources of heat."

He next turned his attention to the *khempo,* who bowed respectfully and said something in Tibetan.

Then the child-leader of the *gompa* turned to Edouard and spoke almost apologetically. "He asks me to leave so that he can begin with you at once. In your own interest." Bowing again at both Edouard and Ugen Rimpoche, he turned and stooped down to re-enter the connecting corridor. In a moment, he was out of sight and Edouard was saying, "I am most honored."

"No, no," Ugen Rimpoche interrupted. He directed a small, mottled hand toward the section of earthen wall that framed the right side of the big window. "What is that?" he demanded unexpectedly.

Edouard, standing awkwardly before the old man, turned to stare for a moment before he replied. "I see only a wall, Rimpoche."

"Wall?" Ugen Rimpoche sounded as though he had never heard the word. "What is wall?"

And all at once, Edouard knew that his instruction had begun. He settled in a squatting position before the old man as though he felt this was the proper thing to do.

"What is wall?" Rimpoche asked again.

"Something you use to enclose a space, to create an inside as opposed to an outside," Edouard replied.

"How do you go outside from the inside created by this thing you call wall?"

"You also build a door, or a corridor leading in from outside the wall."

"Very wasteful," Rimpoche said, pursing his thin, colorless lips. "Is there no better way to get back outside?"

"Not unless you can go through walls," Edouard suggested with a hint of annoyance.

"Ah. Why not?"

Startled, Edouard considered for a moment. "Well, given the molecular structure of matter—"

"No, no," Rimpoche interrupted. "You are chemist. So you understand, from being chemist, that when you go below molecular level, subatomic level, some of the things that make wall solid, they disappear. Is there heat at subatomic level? No. You understand that, surely?"

"Yes, but I don't understand your point."

"I will now make such point. I urge you consider that as you increase complexity, the more barriers you create. As you go from subatomic to molecular level, suddenly there appears heat. Yes?"

"Well, yes."

"That is chemical law. Indeed, universal law. The higher you go in complexity, the more barriers you create because you have more, more structures, yes? You have more structures from which emerge properties not originally present. You must remove such structures from your mind. As the phrase goes, get down to basics, yes?"

Edouard frowned. He was following the logic of it now but he still had serious doubts.

"No, no," the old man said. "You will not walk through walls, because there are no walls. You will simply walk where you please. Some choose to call it walking through walls, but strictly speaking you no longer have perception of walls. That is surely very clear?"

Edouard placed his fingertips on the center of his forehead and made a wiping movement toward the left and the right as though removing the mental cobwebs that veiled his understanding. "Clear? Yes, Rimpoche. It's clear. But, I'm not sure it's right."

"With proper exercises, clarity will reveal rightness." Again, the old monk indulged in a brief birdlike chuckle. "Similarly," he went on, "you will learn that space can be diminished, mountains can be reduced in scale, and you will have secret of *lon-gompa*."

The old man rose all at once from his seat, sliding lightly off the cushions with an alacrity that surprised his visitor. "Your concentration will be limited. On that I must warn you. Before we begin."

"And why is that, Rimpoche?"

"It takes many years of mind training to achieve *lon-gompa*. You will not have time enough. Your ability to hold the mind-state will perhaps get you to Minya Konka. But after that, in the absence of longer discipline, your concentration will weaken. You will be unable to return." He gazed somberly at Edouard. "A one-way trip. You understand?"

For a long time, Edouard was silent. Then he said, "What I need to do is at Minya Konka. There is nothing I have to bring back."

"Aah. How do you know that?"

Edouard frowned. "It has something to do with what happened back on the trail. When one of us—Horgan—had this dream, or thought it was a dream. He was reading a Batman comic to his son. They must have told you. When he came out of the hypoxia, he had killed three men. Except that I was—" He paused, uncertain about how to relate himself to that sense of other identities with whom he now knew himself to be involved.

It was the old monk who now asked the key question. "But the need of these other personalities, this Alvin. And this Horgan. Why do you take on their burdens?"

"Because I am certain that what I must do at Minya Konka, well, the fate of the entire planet depends on it."

"Fate of planet depends on what everyone does," the old man replied dryly.

"You're telling me not to go, then?"

"Of course you must go. It is what you are." Then he added in response to Edouard's puzzled look, "All three of your other personalities—you form—how to say it best?—yes, form a cluster of value. Value has to do with the way things come together." He smiled suddenly. "Correction. The way things come together has to do with value. There is a difference."

The old monk was standing directly in the chrome yellow light that the fading sun still poured through the window. He looked for a moment to Edouard like an icon of brass. For some seconds, Edouard stared at the mysterious old man, entranced. Then, recollecting himself, "You mention an additional person. Who is that?"

"He was created here in Tibet."

"Created?"

"That is how I read the forces I see around you. Yes, created. You know what a *tulpa* is?"

"Yes, in fact. I do. But how does he—?"

"Through Alvin. And also by necessity. A triangle needs three sides. And value is a triangle."

"Rimpoche, I confess, you confuse me. A triangle?"

"Meaning always works by threes. Otherwise, how would you know right from left? Up from down? Truth from falsehood? Where is the reference point? Do you understand why I say all these things so strange to your ears? It is how I say, yes, it is right. You must go. And soon. Everything appears to be in place. So, we must start at once."

"And how do we do that?"

"I will tell you what to do. And you will do it."

Chapter Eighteen

"I remember, I remember," Kay said excitedly. "He was saying the same thing that Thongden said to you when—"

"Yes, the very same thing. In the multilayered universe, as it really exists, there are clumps of events that belong together, that are related in a kind of noncausal grouping, their connection having to do with value and meaning rather than material events. How can I forget? It was all so completely tied together. It's stamped in memory as indelibly as some of the poems I learned in childhood."

"That's a strange association. Why would you bring up childhood in such a context?"

"Oh, come on. It was just a simile." And then I considered for a moment. Kay had an exquisite sensitivity for nuances like this. Was I missing something? "You know, I was thinking of my old explorer friend, Joe Spinden, the one who first found the lost cities and then translated the Mayan codex. About the time he had that argument with the children's analyst, when he tried to make the point that children really could fly. For an instant, I had this memory of Joe as he made statements that completely confused the analyst, what was his name?—from Columbia University—Bela Mittelman. Anyway, that's the connection. Children flying. *Lon-gompa* is the same thing, in a way. I mean, it's the same thing that children do. And that's what Edouard did. He became a child. He had a child mind. No preconceptions. I mean, rather, to put it more psychologically, if you like, he had been reduced to very limited apperceptions."

"I don't know what in the world you're talking about," Kay said.

I sat down in the armchair facing the couch and folded my hands. It was as though I were Ugen Rimpoche telling Edouard all over again that he had too many structures. "You see, as we grow and learn, we structure our world. And while that gives us a world to move around in, it also limits us. Children don't have such structures. They have pretty direct perception, thanks to the absence of learned ideas and notions about the world. So their apperceptions are limited. That's what the exercises did for Edouard: limited his apperceptions. So he was free to think himself where he wanted to go. Up to a point, of course. You see, they put him through those breathing exercises and meditations. A process of freeing his consciousness of its acquired notions of reality. But it was a very hasty and jerry-rigged kind of teaching, as Ugen Rimpoche had warned. But it gave him the capacity to get there anyway. It made it possible for him to march straight to Minya Konka despite mountains and freezing temperatures. He did it almost exactly the way children fly. Actually, he did fly, using his feet and his imagination too, so that he could scale down the difficulties."

"You sound very sure of all this," Kay said, still skeptical.

"I remember it, that's why. I was there. In fact, so were the other three—the whole triangle. But Edouard was the one onstage. And he simply followed the path he'd worked out by his remote sensing analyses for adramacite. Do you remember, that's what sent him there in the first place? He was looking for adramacite? And that's how he brazenly climbed up the frozen glaciated face of Minya Konka and found the cave. And that was as far as his training at the monastery could take him.

"In Edouard's mind, the way it was happening—the way it appeared to his consciousness, was like this." And I went on to describe it in Edouard's words.

I myself did not move. I was the recipient of motion. Wherever I passed, the surface of things carried me. The rocks, the ice melting under the sunlight, extended their energies. A transfer from one part of nature to another, from the slabs of exposed rock, the frail lichens growing on the solar side, from the molecules that shaped and structured and striated the crystalline frozen outer garment of the great mountain, it all came to me. I became motion. I became wings, I became endless numbers of feet, of currents and winds, of thrusts bursting from the moiling earth herself in the great exchange with which my mind was now locked, endlessly focused and sustained in a vast chordal resonance.

Time had folded itself into a Möbius strip, ever back on its own passage, emerging constantly out of its own burgeoning present as it spiraled through the moments to come, the motion of it became part of my own life's motion, returning on me and drawing me forward. I was time's arrow and time itself the motionless bourne through which I passed.

Below the vast cave itself, reinforced by a long slab of rock jutting like a marquee from the gaping tunnel that must have been the entrance, I moved hand over hand, climbed on all fours like a mountain goat to bring myself level with its edge. And then they were on every side of me, the soldiers. Two of them helped me up as I rose above the last two feet, strong arms in gray winter uniforms, pulling me into their midst with a medley of terse raucous commands in Han Chinese. I understood none of it. Yet it seemed I was being welcomed in some manner, more as a guest than a prisoner. But it was impossible to be sure. In either case, it seemed they had been expecting me.

Chapter Nineteen

*The Chinese have always recognized a magical link
between man and the landscape. They see the world
and themselves as part of a sacred metabolic system.
Everything in it pulses with life and each thing depends
on everything else. Nature reacts to change and that
reaction resounds in man. When the earth is healthy
and prospers, we thrive. When the balance is destroyed,
we suffer. Our fate is inextricably bound up with the
cycles of heaven and earth and with the flow of the
weather. And at the root of all things lie the twin forces
of wind and water, feng and shui. So all health and
prosperity depend on the maintenance of harmony
between these forces.*

—LYALL WATSON

"Yes," the small man said, his rendering of English shaped to the nasalities of whatever Chinese dialect he spoke. "You are most welcome. Your presence brings true joy." Very likely Mandarin, I decided from his courtly style. His lined face, and a frame shrunk beyond the ability of his crisply tailored general's uniform to camouflage, seemed decidedly unmilitary. His voice continued in a monotone, almost like a chant scaled in a range too narrow for my Western ears to detect the intervals. He looked ageless, with a face that was all shadows, almost formless, as though invisible layers of gauze masked his features. Probably this was an effect of the huge chamber itself where I sat facing him after the soldiers who brought me had left, except for a young officer who lingered watchfully behind me. It was, at first glance, a spacious, well-appointed, literally cavernous office space. There were desks and chairs and even a set of mainframe computers, actually antiquated IBM 360s. And the light seemed to spread all over, reflected from the stippled white clay walls but coming from overhead where my upward glance revealed a brilliantly phosphorescent rock ceiling.

Strong phosphorescent light plays tricks on the eyes. For an instant everything appears clear to the panoramic glance. Then, as you try to focus on specific objects, they seem to shift. They evade you; and this is especially the case with the human face. That's why my impression of the man who was interviewing me seemed so odd. Until it occurred to me that I probably looked equally murky to him. Adding to the confusion was the intermittent but shattering clash of what sounded like some sort of machine, one that started up at brief intervals with an abrupt, deep clanking and thrusting sound, almost like some gargantuan subterranean creature's heavy breathing, then stopped until, after a time, as though the silence were too unbearable—or the whatever thing needed to take breath again—it started once more. My rational mind inferred that some massive, well-digging contraption was operating deep inside the cave. In a cave? Why?

The old man had continued speaking to me, ignoring the noise that was drowning him out. Only when a soldier stepped forward and thrust a small wooden chair under me, did I realize that he'd been trying to tell me to sit down, and that he was also trying to explain the background noise to me. In the silence that followed, the old man's voice became clear again.

"You comprehend ancient Chinese art of wind and water, feng shui?" he asked unexpectedly. "The great sounds that assault your attention," he went on, gesturing quickly, "—our invocation to feng shui. I am General only of this military phase of operation. But chosen because I am last of great sorcerers of China." And suddenly, his striated cheeks crumpled into a broad smile. His open mouth flashed a row of bright artificial teeth. Abruptly, the clattering started again and I couldn't hear the rest of his sentence. Then he seemed to become aware of the noise and fell silent. At the next hiatus, he addressed the soldier standing behind me in a style of utterance that seemed to confirm my guess about Mandarin being his true tongue. The soldier then shouted toward the far end of the cavern in what I recognized as the ruder sounds of Han Chinese. Echoes of a reply swirled back from the phosphorescent depths, and suddenly, everything in the cave became really silent. I realized that a low hum that had persisted uninterruptedly from the moment I got here had also ceased, allowing me, only now, to become aware of it. The sudden silence was truly startling. Even more startling was the voice of the old man breaking it as he addressed me again. "Now, without interruption, we may exchange thoughts. You had question for me?"

Not one but dozens of questions, I told him. Why had they been expecting me? Had I really been hearing the sound of a great drill back there? What were they looking for in this cave? Had I actually heard the word *sorcerer* when he'd described himself? Did that have something to do with what he called feng shui? And most important of all, if I were welcome here, why had the Chinese authorities refused my request to come here and examine the adramacite I was after, even when I was prepared to pay handsomely for it?

"I am pleased to answer you," the old man said. "Point by point. Most significant point for you, I will explain later." He swiveled back in his chair, clasping his tiny gnarled hands on his lap. "I am Lee Lo Wang. I am sorcerer in sense of mastery of feng shui. I tell you now that I have affection for West in my heart because Harvard University was so kind to accept my oldest son as student. From him, I learn English. But most in my heart is great ancient land of China." He paused, his eyes glinting at me as though he needed to see how I was reacting.

"Yes," I managed. "Your son taught you English. And you love the West but you love China better."

"I have communed with ancestors from whom I inherit long tradition of sorcery. Can you accept such a reality with your Western mind?"

I nodded. "More than you can imagine," I declared.

"Even narrow-thinking Party officials dare not disavow ancient tradition." The old man here raised his hands from his lap in an unmistakable gesture of deprecation. "Reason why? Because China is land of great thirst. Party builds dams, digs canals, causes great Yangtze Valley floods. But most of West does not understand that China still suffers from lack of water. Problem will only get worse. Arid lands will be deserted. Cities will suffer floods of thirsty people." He tittered slightly at his play on words, clearly proud of his English.

I nodded. "I'm very aware of China's great water shortages and the sufferings they've brought. However, you're right; most Westerners perhaps think that water is in excess supply, with the frequent Yangtze floods. But you can't be drilling for water in this cave."

"Precisely yes," Lee Lo Wang surprisingly replied. "But only as a sorcerer drills, a master of feng shui."

And then he started to explain about his extraordinary plan. "In my own ancestral tradition," Lee went on, pausing to light a cigarette, "we do not see earth as a mechanical system to be tormented and deformed and mined for her treasures. Rather is she a living being of which wind and water are but the outer raiment of a living system. So, through this great Minya Konka cavern that stretches deep within the mountain, I have located the main artery, whose blood feeds heart of our land, the nourishing aorta of all China. You are chemist. So you will not be too surprised to learn that the heart of Minya Konka is filled with hematite."

"Ah, yes, I know that. Our research told me that."

"But chemistry and remote sensing cannot truly explain about hematite. You know only that hematite is red iron oxide. Yes and no. You cannot understand how forty-five thousand years ago, men came to this cave and mined the hematite. You understand? This was thousands of years before so-called Iron Age. These early diggers took iron oxide and smelted it with charcoal, not for making weapons but for sacred ceremonies, to pay tribute to Great Mother, the Earth. Because the red oxide was truly known to them as Blood of Earth. Better than we, they understood this. And so, after ceremonies, they carefully restored the hematite, since to despoil the Great Mother of her blood would bring disaster. You understand?"

The old man's account was getting interesting. I'd heard that similar activities had been confirmed by radiocarbon dating of charcoal remnants in Africa. But what was Lee getting at with this long story?

"So now," he continued, thoughtfully snuffing out his cigarette. "As master of feng shui, I have come to understand ancestors' great mistake." He looked at me as though he expected my reaction to some sort of dramatic point. Had I seen it?

I hadn't a clue.

"Restoring hematite to the cave was great mistake. Hematite is out of place here. Nothing grows from it. No changes in the wind can carry water to dry places while hematite lies deep in cave, a gift from the Great Mother that ancestors never used." He thrust a finger at me. "Tell me, Mister Chemist, what happens if you deposit quantities of hematite into deep waters?"

"All right, that's not complicated. The iron ore oxidizes. The extra oxygen encourages plant growth—"

"Precisely so!" Lee broke in triumphantly. "It encourages plant growth. Abundantly. So, we come to Minya Konka, the holy mountain almost entirely filled with hematite. It is clear, no? We arrange to transfuse whole inside of mountain to special spot we have chosen in Indian Ocean. Millions of tons. Plants will then grow there in profusion, yes? Growth warms the air, yes? The winds pick up unaccustomed warmth and change direction, yes? And carry the warm moisture to China's arid provinces. You see?"

I sat for some moments wondering how to tell him I did not see. That he had no way of knowing what kind of change the oxidation would make in the prevailing winds. Why would they necessarily benefit China? Why not India? Why not even worsen the Yangtze floods? I thought these things and realized he was watching me with a quiet smile of certitude.

"Why are you sure the winds will bring the moisture to where China needs it?" I asked finally. "How could you possibly model the possibilities? Even advanced computers couldn't . . ."

He raised a finger. "Now, we leave science behind. Enter at this point, the sorcerer. Myself, the master of feng shui. The diviner of the ways of the wind. You see?"

I stared at him, shrugging.

"Of course you do not see. Like the Party functionaries in Shanghai. They do not see either. But they understand about feng shui. They allow me free hand. And divination tells me the winds will blow where they are needed. So, that is solved. Yes?"

"But, millions of tons. How do you transfuse—you did say transfuse?—all that hematite across so many miles and across national boundaries of countries who might be hurt by changes in wind direction, such as India?"

Lee shrugged. He lit another cigarette. "The subcontinent will be hurt. True, but inevitable. But we do not traverse any boundaries. No, we go under."

And suddenly it became clear to me. Those sounds I'd heard, drilling sounds I thought. I'd been right. Lateral drilling, a technology that the international oil companies had developed and employed for some decades already. But in this case, the activity would be reversed. Instead of drilling to draw petroleum up through their drill holes, Lee and his People's Army cadres had an easier task. All they had to do was send the hematite down into the earth and then laterally across into, most likely, the Bay of Bengal. Which meant that the hematite would first have to be heated and sent as molten slag down and then across, through the lateral tunnels. But then, I realized, they'd have to have a way of keeping the slag hot as it poured all that distance to its undersea outlet. How had they managed to solve that one? And if they *had* solved it, the earth's wind patterns really *could* be disrupted. India as well as dozens of other nations around the globe could go dry. Loss of water would destroy crops on the subcontinent, and starvation would afflict millions. Chinese prosperity would ensue, at the expense of inestimable numbers of neighboring populations.

Lee must have read my thoughts about keeping the slag hot, not a difficult task since the question of temperature maintenance would have occurred to anyone with even a minimal technical background.

"Thin pipes, of a far higher melting point than iron," Lee began, then paused to see if I could figure out the rest of it. I wasn't sure, and said so.

"Because you do not know of volcanic leftovers below Minya Konka, natural gas deposits deep down below this very spot. You see now? This natural gas we send through lines of a special alloy within the drill tunnel where it will automatically inject every few feet into the slag as it pours through. Igniting automatically in proximity to the slag, the gas will maintain the necessary molten temperature. You see, we have worked out everything."

"Except," I grudgingly could not help responding, "about how your hematite will affect the prevailing winds."

Lee laughed lightly. "Your mechanically fixated thought process cannot accept ancient truths of feng shui, of which the power of divination is major aspect. But of all techniques we use here, divination is the most certain."

Chapter Twenty

As Kay listened, I could see her eyes begin to glaze over as I went into the technical details of lateral drilling and temperature maintenance for the slag. But if I hadn't told her all that, she wouldn't have been able to understand what was to follow. At the moment, though, only one thought seemed to stay with her. She reminded me of it now. "I'm still waiting to hear the important part."

"What important part? I thought I was telling you the important part."

"No, no, I mean, when Lee told you . . ." She broke off and waved her arms somewhat helplessly. "I mean told Edouard—how can I keep from getting the different personalities mixed up? You say you were aware of Alvin, or Edouard was—"

"Yes, well?"

"When Lee said the most important point for you, he'd explain last. What was that?"

"Ah, that. Well, I was coming to that. Kind of confusing actually. I'm not sure how to put it. Because I thought Thongden set me up, or rather, set Edouard up. See, you've got me mixing us up too. For obvious reasons. Lee told Edouard, not right away, but after he took him deeper into the cave to see the gas wells and the giant drills. The place was vast. Picture Grand Central Station. Bigger than that. It had to be, to move in all the machinery, the piping. They had to use helicopters to do some of it because of the terrain around Minya Konka. And the People's Republic didn't even have those until they wheedled them out of a consortium of Western oil companies who were doing exploration in another part of China. Lee never told them what it was really for, of course. But, anyway, Edouard was impressed. Lee wanted to impress Edouard because, Edouard realized, the old man liked him. Don't ask me why. But he wanted to postpone the bad news as long as possible. But when they got back again to Lee's office, he told Edouard straight out."

"Edouard?"

"Bazenrüd. Edouard. But by this time, I was so much on the surface of Edouard's consciousness that he was as aware of me by then as I was of him. Except, as I explained, I couldn't do anything. It was his stage. Anyway, Lee sat Edouard down again and started to talk about Thongden. Edouard was mystified. But I knew. And I think maybe I managed to make him aware after Lee went on for a while. Thongden, the *tulpa* created by a certain British Lama, he informed Edouard, was a spy for the rebellious province of Tibet. A dangerous enemy who had to be destroyed. Did Edouard know that he was sharing his mind with another personality? As I explained, Edouard knew that. And he acknowledged it. He was aware of me, Alvin. He had no reason to deny it. But what had this to do with this *tulpa*, Thongden, he asked.

"Lee explained that Thongden's existence depended on Alvin's holding him in thought. He went into some detail until Edouard grasped it. And then came the bombshell. To destroy Thongden, Lee explained, it was only necessary to destroy Alvin. And to destroy Alvin, it was, most regretfully, necessary to destroy Edouard. And Edouard suddenly understood the whole incredible thing. Remember, he hadn't been expecting to make it back safely anyway. But now he knew that the Chinese intended to execute him. That was the unpleasant detail Lee had been saving for last."

"My God!" Kay exclaimed. "Could they have done that? Could they have killed you by killing Edouard? You weren't really there, after all."

I shook my head. "I don't know. At least, I didn't know then. But I found out later that very likely they could have."

"But how did you find that out?"

"How? From Everett Nelson himself, the Englishman who first created Thongden by months of meditation. He said that the bleedthrough into the Edouard Bazenrüd personality had been so complete that I had virtually no other ground to fall back on. What I mean is, Edouard had become the focus of my consciousness. Except for one factor. But I'll get to that. The main thing is, Edouard had to be eliminated. Although at that moment, when I heard Lee explain it, I couldn't understand why Thongden—who knew they were anxious to kill him—ever put me in reach of his Chinese enemies. From what he told me, the whole idea was to frustrate their efforts to kill him. As I say, I was confused. Very confused. Until much later." I stopped suddenly and studied her. "You look tired. I mean, very tired. Sure you want to hear the rest of this right now?"

"You try to postpone this story," Kay replied, "and I'll use my own powers of divination to have you struck by lightning. Will you please go on?"

As it had been all along, it was easier to continue in Edouard's own words, especially in light of the fact that it was he who had to deal with the problem of our joint extinction. As I said, it was his stage.

I was carrying a lot of baggage. I, Edward Horgan, turned Edouard Bazenrüd, plus an Alvin consciousness, plus a thought creature or *tulpa* of Alvin's, the mysterious Tibetan monk, Thongden. This last, I had no awareness of whatsoever, even if Alvin did. Yet because I carried him somehow through the Alvin-consciousness that had bled through to me, I was to be executed. To get at Thongden. Not exactly fair, I thought. But then, when did I ever believe in fairness?

"It's really not fair, you know," I told Lee anyway, wondering if maybe he might still possibly be persuaded to consider some less absolute alternative. The old man was back behind his desk, watching me through an odd canny wrinkling of his eyelids. "Of course, fair," he said in a quite friendly manner. "Because not personal. Is it fair when truck hits you when crossing street? You see, nothing to do with fair. Unpleasant, yes. But more for me than you, my friend." It was the first time he'd called me friend, I realized.

He went on to add, "To me falls unpleasant task involving service to my country. But for you, I assure you, it happens in a most pleasant way."

"What does that mean?" I asked with as much surliness as I could muster.

"It will be pleasure for you," he said, giving me another of his toothy smiles. "Come, we will return to interior of cavern where you can watch the activities. Discover the details of great work that you missed when first I showed you in there. As a man of technology and science, you will appreciate even more . . ."

"You mean," I snapped, "that I'll sit there and watch the whole technical show with such delight, I won't care about getting exterminated? I don't know what you're talking about, General." I put a strong negative emphasis on that military title of his as he spoke. But he wasn't ruffled.

He rose. "Not quite. You will drink concoction I personally will give you. Very interesting concoction. Everything becomes clearer. Your enjoyment of the great engineering spectacle will be enhanced. And so—" Two soldiers seized my arms from behind, as Lee added, "—you will discover state of great enjoyment as you leave us. But now, we must proceed."

The soldiers began guiding my resistant steps back toward the cavern's interior as Lee, walking alongside me, continued to reassure me that he was handling the matter with great thoughtfulness and concern for my well-being.

And then I found myself sitting in the midst of all that clanking machinery, the pipes, the glow of the great furnace farther down the corridor, the great drill whooshing slowly up and down just ten yards from where I sat with my hands strapped to the arms of the sturdy wooden chair they had brought for me and Lee still standing alongside me, wearing what now seemed like a permanent friendly grin— or was it a grimace?—while he held in his hand what looked like an ordinary glass of water. But I knew it wasn't water. Without wasting time, he held it out to me, thrusting it toward my mouth. They were apparently in a great hurry to get this nasty thing over with. As though somehow, even though Thongden was not actually present in any solid form, they feared him. "Drink," Lee ordered, pressing the glass to my lips. "I would dislike something so unfriendly as forcing you."

I had no choice. I hadn't accomplished anything by coming here. But it had been my risk. And I hadn't expected to survive anyway, as I said. I was too proud to start making a fuss now, when it wouldn't do any good anyway. I drank the stuff. I took it down in a single long draft. I kept my mind shut against the thought that I'd never see Lorraine again, or ever have any contact with my son, Jack. Why make it more painful than it was?

To my astonishment, the drink had no taste. None. Was it plain water, after all? A psychological trick of some sort? I sat there, watching Lee, waiting for something to happen. But nothing happened at all. Not a thing. Seconds passed. Then minutes. Still nothing happening. But, something was happening to Lee. He was shrinking. Small and wizened as he was, he was becoming even smaller, and younger looking. And familiar. Very familiar.

Eric was wearing the small pea cap he liked to put on at a somewhat rakish angle when we went outdoors on the deck and I sat in the canvas recliner and read to him. This wasn't a story I particularly liked. But, as usual, when I disliked something, Eric seemed to like it. Eric? My son's name was Jack. Jack Schwartz? No, no—Horgan. But who was Horgan? My son's name was Eric. Eric Schwartz. It was Eric who wore a pea cap. Kay encouraged him to wear it because she had this idea his hair was so fine that it didn't really protect his head from the ultraviolet. Funny, I had this idea I wasn't myself. For a moment, I was remembering someone named Edward Horgan. Was that it? Horgan? Or Morgan? Did it matter?

Eric was pressing me to get on with the story. I really didn't like it much after all this time. But since I'd written it, I could change it. The original action had been taking place in a cave, the Batcave. One of those gimmicks I felt went too far. Bill Finger, who had created Batman with Bob Kane, had invented the Batcave. Bill was unusually good on Batman. But sometimes too hokey for my taste. What about a phosphorescent cave deep inside a mountain where this old Chinese sorcerer had been meditating for years, and he had such powers that Batman just lay there paralyzed. He lay there on the rough stone floor not far away from the huge boiling cauldron, which the old man had kept heated by his meditative powers. Also it powered the giant drilling machinery that was operating in the center of the cave, making a long underground passageway that would give him a getaway to the sea. Batman knew he had to stop him.

But finally, as the old man came close, Batman abandoned his pretense of being helpless and paralyzed by Lee's powers. He had found out all he wanted to know. He seized the startled wizard and hurled him into his own superheated cauldron. He smashed the giant drill by levering it up from its moorings with a long steel beam, and suddenly a rushing, screaming sound of released air and gases rose from the long drill hole. Batman felt himself being hurled out of the cave, landing on soft snow on the flank of the great mountain.

And then, with the aid of his Batropes and his Batwings, he was able to traverse vast snowy distances, manage steep drops. Thinking all the time that if Bill was hokey, this was really going him one better. Did I really want to continue with this story?

Chapter Twenty-One

"You see?" I asked Kay as she sat fixed to her place on the couch, watching me in the same way that I now remembered Eric used to watch me when I'd read him an especially exciting comic, "You see?"

She shook her head. "See what?"

"All along, Thongden knew what he was doing. When he sent me into the jaws of the tiger, so to speak. I mean, he was counting on his ace in the hole."

"Such as what?"

"Batman's rage. He knew that there was some risk in sending Bazenrüd into a situation where he'd fall into the hands of the sorcerer, Lee. But what Lee didn't know about, and Thongden did, was another element that had taken hold in my personality. One that had been part of me for years, that accounted for my tendency to lose money, a way of turning a long-suppressed anger on myself. What was it? Batman's rage. The element into which I projected all my own pent-up anger all the years I wrote for DC Comics. The reason I never really liked working on Batman. There's more. About where the anger came from. But anyway, Thongden was counting on the possibility that under extreme pressure, that Batman rage I carried in me would explode and destroy Lee's operation and get Bazenrüd free, along with the Alvin personality who sustained Thongden. Isn't that clear now?"

"Like mud," Kay said.

I was crestfallen, but decided to keep it to myself for now. Maybe by the time I explained the rest of it, she'd understand. In fact, as I considered it, how could it be clear to her? There were still important pieces to be added.

"Anyway, it was that terrible rage that helped me survive Lee's concoction. And the power of it got me all the way back to the Yellow Hat monastery. They found me lying in the snow a few yards from the entrance."

"In your Batman costume?" Kay sounded her skeptical best.

"Come on, you know that was all imaginary," I said. "No, they found Edouard Bazenrüd, of course. And while, as Edouard, I remembered what had happened at Minya Konka, I couldn't be sure that I'd destroyed things there in reality or merely imagined it too. But Ugen Rimpoche made all that clearer after I'd had a few hours of much-needed rest."

"Now, to remind you about earlier question concerning wall," Rimpoche said. "Consider great anger that lives with a man for many years. After a time, anger itself is like a wall. Maybe even it builds several walls, and a man is their prisoner all this lifetime. In West, there are sometimes psychotherapists who help dissolve such walls. It takes sometimes many years. What do they do? They go back into causes. Bad parents. Bad experiences. In fact, there are no such causes. Only in comic books. Like Batman. In real world, chronic anger develops from nowhere. The cause may be flutter of a butterfly's wing. This moves the air. Random changes in air get picked up by passing currents and become magnified. A storm builds. Whole villages are destroyed. You understand? Are these causes or something else? Like changing shapes of passing clouds, perhaps? So why do Western therapists sometimes succeed? Most times, they fail. But sometimes they succeed because, without realizing it, they lead patient to walk through walls. Did I not teach you to walk through walls?" And suddenly, as I sat there trying to answer that one, he broke into a soft melodic laugh and waved a hand at me. "No matter. I am only wing of butterfly. But this time, butterfly destroys the evil at Minya Konka. In the end, of course, your real strength," he added, "comes from the great *lon-gompa* energy you acquired. The Batman personality was only the trigger—or better still, the inspiration."

"You're sure of that?" I asked. "It was really destroyed?"

"I am sure, because you returned here. I did not expect that. Because I expected nothing from your Batman fantasies. And I hadn't counted on the *lon-gompa* carrying you over so long. What will you do now?"

"Home," I said. "I'll go home."

"Good. Jean-Marc Robillard is still here with your team. He more than I was sure you would return. He and Sherpas will get you back. I am this time most sure."

And of course, they did get me back. I thought Lorraine would be overwhelmed, delighted, thrilled to see me and hear what I had to tell her.

And so it turned out—from the prologue that so joyfully annulled our long-postponed intimacy to the hours of talk that followed. Then, profoundly entwined around one another, we slept.

It was late morning and we were still in bed when I first tried to remind Lorraine that my trip to Minya Konka was really the culmination of all our work. The destruction of the great evil we had been concerned about.

"Always there is great evil to put our energies into," she told me somewhat brusquely as she slid out from between the covers and began dressing. Last night's mood had vanished. She clearly had something else on her mind. "You are rested enough now, I hope?"

"That's a strange question. Why do you ask that?"

"I would not want us to go to England when you are too tired."

"England?"

"Her Majesty. You have surely not forgotten the investiture?"

"But it really doesn't matter that much anymore," I protested.

"To me it matters very much," Lorraine said firmly. She yanked at the covers. "Get up."

I struggled over and sat on the side of the bed. "But, why?"

"Why? I cannot explain why the way you wish. But my being a strong woman, as we both know I am, does not mean there is no more the little girl in me. The same little girl, you should understand, that makes me the kind of woman I am. And the little girl wants her lover to be also her knight. That is all I can tell you. If you refuse me, I will abandon you forever."

"Well," I said, starting to get dressed. "If you feel that way about it, let's go to England."

I didn't realize the time was so short. We couldn't wait for a regular flight. So we had to charter a flight. We barely managed to make it.

In due course, we turned up at Buckingham Palace, with Lorraine in a formal gown that adorned a beauty that had never been as brilliantly present during all of her long film career. It was as though this occasion was her final blazoning forth, a rite of passage through which her public self would pass once and for all into a profound privacy, to cast off, in the process, all that baggage of her past which I had already discarded from mine.

Even before I went through the experience of appearing before Her Majesty, kneeling, being touched by the tip of her ceremonial sword, I felt as though I were being newly certified, newly accoutered in a selfhood that was fully and finally mine. Perhaps it was the sheer weight of eleven centuries of tradition, in which the doughty spirits of forty generations, a span of time particularly impressive to an American for whom history began less than two centuries ago, were somehow gathered in the royal hand holding that ceremonial weapon. Perhaps too it was a contagion of feeling from Lorraine's own deep commitment to the occasion that moved me so much. But, in any case, rising, I intercepted those eyes of Her Majesty the Queen upon me. And I had the strangest feeling that she recognized me. A recognition that had nothing to do with Horgan or Bazenrüd but was more intrinsic, since it had the effect of certifying me to myself. And then she startled me by speaking to me as if the rigid and ancient ceremony had been merely an elaborate excuse for a quick personal exchange.

"We are very grateful for your services in the Falklands affair, Sir Edouard."

I managed to respond with a nod and a few polite words. "It was hardly possible to refuse such a request from Your Majesty." The Alvin in me seemed to be tittering deep down inside. This being a special European thing, how could an American like Alvin have appreciated it? As for Horgan, he had lived in Europe now for so long that he had become thoroughly Europeanized.

But now, Her Majesty confronted me with a knowing smile; yes, it really was a confrontation, in the form of a very personal response and accompanied by words equally startling, "But was it simply a talent of yours for handling such matters, or a service to some deeper cause?"

"Will you accept it as a service to Your Royal Highness, Majesty?" I managed to reply.

"We already have," she announced. "But I, personally, should like to know more about why you really did it. Is that possible?"

"Just the normal course of business, actually."

"Oh no, it was not normal. But then, we presume it's a trade secret and we must not press you."

"Your Majesty, it is indeed a trade secret. And I shall be happy to share it with you at some appropriate future time."

"We shall take you up on that, be certain, Sir Edouard. Indeed, there's no time like the present." And smiling, she urged me to go straight ahead into the next room. "Right behind the arras," she said, pointing. "There's somebody waiting for you."

"For me?"

"No more questions. Just please go."

I managed to exchange a puzzled glance and a shrug with Lorraine, who stood watching over to my left. Then, as Her Majesty had ordered, I moved on past her and pulled aside the arras to find it concealing a small sitting room dominated by a single great portrait of some unfamiliar eighteenth-century nobleman. The room's only occupant turned away from the window and came toward me with outstretched hand. He was a tall, slightly stooped man of perhaps seventy, with a face deeply seamed by years of rugged outdoor exposure, like an old mountain climber. In fact, there was something about his weathered face that reminded me of our recent Sherpa guide, although there was certainly no resemblance. "How fortunate for me, to be able to meet you, at last," he said. His hand took mine and held it for a moment as he peered into my eyes. "I'm Everett Nelson, Sir Edouard. And may I add that in your person, I am also meeting a guest of yours? A certain bleedthrough tenant. Are you aware of Alvin at this moment?"

"Everett Nelson?" I repeated, puzzled. At the same time, I began to sense that the name was indeed known to me. Not directly. But, as I became aware of Alvin's presence, I began to understand who Everett Nelson was. The creator of Thongden. Which also explained Her Majesty's cryptic questions. Nelson must have told her a good deal. I looked at this remarkable man with a touch of awe. Perhaps it was Alvin's lurking presence that contributed some of that feeling.

"This is a surprise, and quite an honor, Dr. Nelson." And then, out of my now solidly acquired Bazenrüdish aplomb, I asked, "And before I lose the opportunity, can you answer the one question that troubles me: could my, well, my bleedthrough guest, Alvin, have been killed by the sorcerer through my death?"

Nelson smiled. He motioned me to a seat, settled himself in one of the ancient, beautifully preserved brocaded chairs, and said, "You could really answer that yourself if you understood one thing. I suppose in modern terms, you'd call it the nonlocality of the self."

"Uh-oh," I thought. "Alfred again. More of Ugen Rimpoche's Whitehead."

Imperturbably, Nelson went on, "If the self chooses to localize itself in any specific place or time, as Alvin localized himself in you, well, the answer is yes. Very simple really. Where you are is where you are vulnerable."

I was staring down at the ornate Westminster rug at my feet, noticing that it seemed to get darker as I watched it. Probably some trick of the light. I looked up and said, "Where I am?" And stopped.

"It's all right," a different voice said. "It's time."

I was looking at Thongden. Back in his office, inside the room with the mirror. Yes, it was like waking from a dream.

"You really had no more business with our friend Edouard. So I brought you back," he explained.

I sat for some moments, gripping the arms of my chair as I watched him. "A dream," I said finally, and gripped the chair some more. "Or something a lot like it. . . . Well, it was . . . interesting."

Thongden smiled very broadly and nodded. He looked pleased. "You're not angry?" he asked.

"Why should I be angry?"

"Usually, when I'm up to one of my tricks, as you call them, you do get angry. Why not this time?"

"As I recall," I explained patiently, "you were supposed to be working on my anger. The thing that was making me lose money. Batman's rage, you called it."

"Correct. So is it possible I succeeded?"

"Because I'm not angry now?" I said dubiously.

"I suppose," Thongden began, getting up from his seat, and turning the dimmer switch on the wall to raise the lights, "that in future, if all this works out, you won't be so consistently losing money on your investments."

I stood up too, rubbing my eyes. "Investments? Oh, that. We'll see, won't we? Anyway, that was some dream." He kept looking at me.

"Well," I added, "if it wasn't a dream, how come they wanted to kill me for keeping you alive when Nelson, your original creator, was still around? I didn't start keeping you alive until Nelson had died."

"I suggest you recall that the time switch took place at a moment when I was being sustained by your thoughts, not my original creator's, even though it might seem that in this crossing of time frames, you might expect that my original creator, Nelson, would have been supporting me. Not necessarily, as there is no way of knowing which one's Thongden would be operating, since you, Alvin, were really an intrusion from the future when you, or rather, Edouard, was meeting Nelson." He rolled it all off as though he'd been elaborately preparing for the question.

I passed a hand across my forehead. "Oh boy. Maybe we'd better go over that again."

Thongden pulled over another chair and settled on it to face me comfortably. "You are here now," he began.

"Of course I'm here now. When else?"

"No, no—*now*. Think about now. Wherever you go, it is now. Wherever you find yourself, it is now. In fact, you could never find yourself except now." He squinted at me as though seeking some kind of gathering realization.

"Yes, all right. I'm here now. What of it? If I weren't here now, I wouldn't be here at all. What's the point?"

"Precisely. Now is a point. Timeless, dimensionless. You can't observe it because, as we know today from our very clever physicists, there is no outside observer. Only now. Now is you. Now is—the observer. Do you understand? You are always and absolutely here and now. In that sense, wherever you are, you are always yourself. You believe Ugen Rimpoche taught you to walk through walls? But there are no walls, not now." And he gave one of his sudden self-delighted chortles. "Because, you see, everything you are and remember, is now."

"And the future?"

"Could there be a future without a now?" He paused briefly, stroked his chin and waited for my response.

I squirmed in the chair as the whole idea began to bore in on me. I began to feel a strange sense of freedom. But I didn't want to be that free. I felt a need for limits. For some kind of boundaries. I suggested this to him.

"Create all the limits you desire," he said. "That's where the fun comes in. But never forget who created them."

I stood up, suddenly struck by something that had been nagging at me. It was all that talk of limits. "I think I'd better get home first thing. God, I've been away for, how long."

"Four years," Thongden said with a grin. "I've been counting."

Afterword

Kay and I both tried to locate Bazenrüd and Lorraine. The closest we came was to find a reclusive European financier with a "Sir" before his name, which was not Bazenrüd, who happened to be married to a former French actress, with a name very unlike Lorraine. Was this my Edouard, nonetheless? And Edward Horgan? Well, he had covered his tracks pretty well, if there really had been a man of that name. As Steve Jordan recently explained to me, the names would prove least reliable in the recall of such experiences.

"How would you know about something like that?" I asked him.

"The things you first start to forget as you age," he reminded me. "What are they?"

"Names?"

"Of course," Steve said.

And the last time I saw Thongden, all he said was, "It's like that when one moves through parallel worlds." Take adramacite, for example. There simply is no such element. Not in this universe. So a lot of detail remains ambiguous. Thongden took off too one day. No telling where he's likely to show up next.

But interestingly enough, I haven't had any financial losses lately.

In fact, I began to realize that once my so-called Batman rage had faded, I had very little interest in financial matters. I've even arranged to have a financial advisor handle our small investments. I have better things to do with my time. Like trying to keep all those lines in balance, without overdoing it.

About the Author

Alvin Schwartz began his writing career while still in high school during the Little Magazine movement of the 1930s. During his attendance at City College of New York and the University of Chicago, he got to know and was influenced by William Carlos Williams, Gertrude Stein, and other literary luminaries of the day.

He began writing comics for *Fairy Tale Parade* in 1939 and went on to write his first Batman story in 1942 and his first Batman and Superman newspaper strips in 1944. He wrote most of DC Comics' newspaper strips between 1944 and 1952, the Golden Age of Comics. He also briefly took over the Superman radio show for a couple of programs—writing words and music for a double recording venture that became a sellout. Schwartz ended his comic writing days with his creation of Bizarro in 1957—his own effort at deconstructing Superman.

In 1948, Alvin Schwartz published his first novel, *The Blowtop*, described by the *New York Times* as the first conscious existentialist novel in America and regarded as one of the first beat novels, having sparked a whole range of subsequent efforts by such writers as Allen Ginsberg and Jack Kerouac.

ABOUT THE AUTHOR

In 2006 Mr. Schwartz received the Bill Finger* Award for Excellence in Comic Book Writing. He is also winner of the prestigious Canada Council award and has authored three pseudonymous novels for Arco Press, scripted two feature films, and wrote and researched some thirty docudramas for the National Film Board of Canada.

His book *An Unlikely Prophet*, first published in 1997, is a prequel to *A Gathering of Selves*.

---

*Bill Finger was the cocreator with Bob Kane of Batman. This annual award was first established in 2005.

BOOKS OF RELATED INTEREST

An Unlikely Prophet
A Metaphysical Memoir by the Legendary
Writer of Superman and Batman
by Alvin Schwartz

Immortality and Reincarnation
Wisdom from the Forbidden Journey
by Alexandra David-Neel

Tantric Quest
An Encounter with Absolute Love
by Daniel Odier

Don Juan and the Power of Medicine Dreaming
A Nagual Woman's Journey of Healing
by Merilyn Tunneshende

Twilight Language of the Nagual
The Spiritual Power of Shamanic Dreaming
by Merilyn Tunneshende

On the Toltec Path
A Practical Guide to the Teachings of Don Juan Matus,
Carlos Castaneda, and Other Toltec Seers
by Ken Eagle Feather

DMT: The Spirit Molecule
A Doctor's Revolutionary Research into the Biology of
Near-Death and Mystical Experiences
by Rick Strassman, M.D.

A Psychonaut's Guide to the Invisible Landscape
The Topography of the Psychedelic Experience
by Dan Carpenter

INNER TRADITIONS • BEAR & COMPANY
P.O. Box 388
Rochester, VT 05767
1-800-246-8648
www.InnerTraditions.com

Or contact your local bookseller